RED-HOT
Romance
Tips
FOR
WOMEN

BILL & PAM FARREL

HARVEST HOUSE PUBLISHERS
EUGENE, OREGON

Cover design by Left Coast Design, Portland, Oregon; cover photo © szefei / Shutterstock

Bill and Pam Farrel are represented by the literary agency of Alive Communications, Inc., 7680 Goddard Street, Ste. 200, Colorado Springs, CO 80920. www.alivecommunications.com.

RED-HOT ROMANCE TIPS FOR WOMEN
Copyright © 2014 by Bill and Pam Farrel
Published by Harvest House Publishers
Eugene, Oregon 97402
www.harvesthousepublishers.com

ISBN 978-0-7369-5149-4 (pbk.)
ISBN 978-0-7369-5150-0 (eBook)

Printed in the United States of America

13 14 15 16 17 18 19 20 21 22 / BP-JH / 10 9 8 7 6 5 4 3 2 1

BEGINNING YOUR RED-HOT
Romance Journey ♥

I hope you've seen it, felt it, experienced it at least once—that sparkle in your man's eye; that wide, full-toothed bemused grin from ear to ear; that strong arm reaching out to hold you; that hot breath on your neck begging you to come nearer, nearer, nearer; that kiss on the nape of your neck followed by the whisper, "I want you…I need you…I love you…I desire you."

Deep down we women have the desire to be desired, but often we shun the idea of becoming women who are *desirable*. After all, that might require some changes on our part. To become *the* beloved, we might have to *be* loving. "Allure" is a word we often see used in reference to "the pursuit" or early days of a romantic relationship. To achieve the preferred status of being appealing, we have to work on not being annoying, agitating, or aggravating.

Through this book, we're going to explore 26 traits (A to Z) that will help make us desirable, alluring, and sought-after wives. To glean these traits, Bill and I took statements we heard from husbands and studied

them to discern the most common hurts, disappoint-
ments, and pains of men's hearts. Then we explored
how romancing *husbands* might help things from the
wives's side of the equation. (Please check out our website www.Love-Wise.com for a list of the most common
frustrations husbands voice and helpful information on
marriage and romance in marriage.) We turned those
grievances inside out to find the romantic qualities
wives could use to fan the flames on the embers of love.

We'll explore the qualities men find attractive in
women. The best way to fan the flames on love is to
become the irresistible women of our men's dreams!

Bill and I want to be totally upfront with you. We
hold a "natural" view of sexual enhancement and education. We believe that love, sex, and intimacy were
pretty amazing when God created them back in the
time of the Garden of Eden. This means we won't be
encouraging you to buy a suitcase full of sexual toys,
expensive enhancement tools, or employ anything that
might violate the precious secret-and-sacred space of
your marital bed. We also won't be including a discussion on birth control. (We have an exhaustive discussion of that in our book *The First Five Years*.)

The focus of *Red-Hot Romance Tips for Women* is
to help you build *your* originality and ingenuity into
your marriage. There will be plenty of red-hot ideas
shared, but they are meant to be sparks to ignite *your*

imagination. We believe the most erotic spot in your body is your mind. At the core, red-hot romance is not a list of ideas. It is all about relationship!

We've designed this journey to sizzling romance to be simple to follow. There are just 26 entries arranged alphabetically. If you read and apply one each day, in 26 days you could become a new woman: more loving, caring, compassionate, and sexy. You can also space out the application to one a week so that over the course of approximately six months you'll have 26 romantic encounters. We recommend the compressed, 26-days-in-a-row model because it provides several perks:

- ♥ *Focus*—All your time, energy, and thoughts will be aimed at one goal: becoming more desirable.

- ♥ *Freedom*—You will like the woman you are becoming: sexy, sought-after, alluring.

- ♥ *Fine-tuning*—Your essence, your character, your inner heart, and your being will be impacted. You'll become…well, nicer. This book will help sand off any rough edges.

It Is Worth It!

There is no downside to becoming a more alluring woman. As you become more desirable, it does raise the possibility, the chance, the likelihood that your husband will notice the difference and want to spend more time—even more romantic or sexual time—with you. However, in the remote chance that he doesn't respond the way you hope or expect, keep putting your energy into this process. You will like the more confident, skilled, and affectionate woman you will become. *Everyone* in your life will benefit.

KISS It!

Take a moment to write a few goals for what you hope will be the result of the time we'll spend together developing your red-hot romance skills. A strong goal for love should include a KISS:

Knowledgeable—You might have to get out of your comfort zone and do some research and reconnaissance to find the best answers for your situation. We've tried to provide a solid launching pad for your exploration and investigation. What one question do you hope gets answered?

Inspired—Dream grand and attempt greatness on behalf of your man and your marriage. How do you want to feel toward you husband by day 26?

S*pecific*—Nail down the details. Take "a hope" and turn it into a tangible action plan. What one habit of love do you hope happens?

S*cheduled*—Be intentional. Make time for this project. You'll need time to read, time to pray for your man and your marriage, and time for red-hot romance moments and dates. Plan action steps and then write them on your calendar or in your Outlook calendar so you'll get them accomplished. What days and times will you dedicate to this journey toward red-hot love?

Answering these few questions will help you KISS.

Don't Go It Alone

God is with you, and He is the author of love!

Beloved, let us love one another, for love is from God; and everyone who loves is born of God and knows God (1 John 4:7).

God is love, and the one who abides in love abides in God, and God abides in [her] (1 John 4:16).

We love, because [God] first loved us (1 John 4:19).

Yes, God is with you on this journey! Talk to Him about your hopes, dreams, ideas, and feelings. If you hit a tough spot, simply stop and say, "God, show me what to do." He'll plant the seed of an idea, a spark of desire, and give you a glint of hope.

Ask Someone to Help You

You might be braver, more willing, and better able to follow through if you have some accountability. You and a friend, a sister, a mentor, or even a marriage-related Bible-study group can walk this path together. Ask God to let you know who might be willing to go with you on this journey toward being a more loving woman. Then buy her a copy of this book and get started. Or get a group of women and make the trek together toward becoming better wives and lovers. (At www.Love-Wise.com you can get a downloadable discussion guide for this book.)

I (Pam) have seen great power in this "sistering" to encourage each wife to love her husband more faithfully. Bill and I wrote a book called *Red-Hot Monogamy*. It's an 8-week guide to help couples turn up the temperature behind bedroom doors. The book is for a couple to read together, and it includes "hands-on homework" (pun completely intended).

One reader looking for a few ideas to add some sizzle to an already good marriage read it and used many of the creative ideas. Her marriage went from good to great. She led a marriage discussion with a small group of women. Afterward, a woman came up to her in tears because her marriage was unraveling. So the leader gave her friend our *Red-Hot Monogamy* book.

As she read *Red-Hot Monogamy*, her heart warmed toward her husband. After speaking and listening to the Lord an ember of optimism was fanned. This hopeful wife began to call home. Each night she'd share portions of *Red-Hot Monogamy* with her husband. Meanwhile, her husband spruced up their love nest (one of the red-hot romance suggestions).

When the wife returned and saw the *tangible* acts of love and desire on his part, she was impressed. "We've been walking, journaling, doing devotions, and praying together. I have my husband back!"

That is red-hot romance! And it will work for you too! We also encourage you to keep a journal as you go through this book so you can capture the ideas and thoughts these topics generate. Are you ready? Turn the page and start rekindling your love or adding more fuel to the fire.

Appreciative ♥

Becoming a wife who expresses gratitude and recognizes the quality, value, and significance of her man.

You're reading this book because you appreciate your husband and your marriage. Because you love your man, you're looking for creative ideas to keep the spark and sizzle in your love life. In your heart is a desire to help your husband feel like the most fortunate male on the face of the globe because he had the good sense to marry *you*.

One of the basic components of a strong love relationship is when a man feels appreciated, valued, and esteemed. I (Pam) love the look in the eyes of newlywed brides. The gleam in their eyes and the broad smiles shout appreciation! When your husband senses you feel you've won the grand prize when you married him, his heart will definitely be drawn toward you. You become priceless in his eyes! "A good woman is hard to find, and worth far more than diamonds" (Proverbs 31:10 MSG).

Why You?

When *52 Ways to Wow Your Husband: Put a Smile on His Face* was released, one of the first events I had it on sale at was a "women's day," where women from all walks of life came for education, encouragement, and inspiration. Several times that day I heard:

♥ Why me?   ♥ Why is it worth it?

♥ Why not him?   ♥ Why try?

♥ Why "Wow"?

My response was usually "Why not you?" Love has to begin with someone someplace, sometime, and somehow. (And if you're wondering if we let husbands off the hook, fear not. Bill works to equip husbands to romance their wives. Stay connected with us through www.Love-Wise.com, and you'll discover resources that are available for your husband too.)

You can be the spark plug for your marriage—the igniter of romance! That, my dear, is *power*! You're not a doormat, not pathetic, not weak just because you want to be a woman who loves her man or even, dare I say it, a gal who wants to please her guy. That is not weakness—it is strength. Your love toward your husband and your marriage has the power to change your marriage and, yes, perhaps even change *him*. As you change yourself, your change compels a change in the relationship, which may lead to him changing.

If you're married to a husband who abuses you in any way—make sure you and everyone else in your family is physically safe and then read Leslie Vernick's book *The Emotionally Destructive Marriage*. For most of us, however, a little bit of lovin' will go a long way toward improving the atmosphere in our relationships.

∾ Tips for Red-Hot Romance ∾

Say thanks! Choose one of these synonyms of appreciation to tangibly express your gratitude to your man.

- ♥ Through written or spoken praise, let your man know you admire a specific quality he possesses.

- ♥ Applaud a specific effort or accomplishment your man has done.

- ♥ Approve heartily of a particular choice he's made today.

- ♥ Commend him in front of his friends or colleagues.

- ♥ Compliment one of his physical features.

- ♥ Accept one of his quirks with a quick hug or kiss when you see it.

- ♥ Laud one of his accomplishments with a gift or family celebration.

- ♥ Warm toward an idea he's brought up by asking for more details.

- ♥ Support one of his dreams by placing a photo of him doing it on your desk or refrigerator.

- ♥ Adore his body in the bedroom by giving a full-body massage.

- ♥ Enthusiastically embrace one of his opinions. Say, "I so agree with you!"

- ♥ Show pleasure in his company. Say, "It's so nice to have you in my life."

- ♥ Be mindful of one of his needs by running an errand or picking up an item for him without being asked.

- ♥ Order a coffee mug with "I thank God 4 U!" printed on it. Take him breakfast in bed, including coffee in that special mug.

- ♥ Place a thank-you note on a helium balloon and float it into his home office when he's working.

Beautiful ♥

Becoming a wife with qualities that delight and please the senses: lovely, pretty, attractive, gorgeous, exquisite, stunning, elegant, striking, cute, appealing, eye-catching, nice-looking, stylish.

Your husband at some point (and most likely now) would use at least one of the above words to describe you. A story that captures why your man might think you're beautiful (even if you don't feel that way) goes back to the first love story—Adam and Eve.

God grabbed a rib from Adam and made Eve. The word "made" in the Hebrew is *banah*, and it gives the impression of God planning out Eve's design. So if your guy has ever said, "You are the woman of my dreams" or "It's like we were made for each other," he is right! You were and are designed for him.

As we discuss beauty, can we agree to set aside the unrealistic runway model expectations? That's a relief because "80 percent of women in the U.S. are dissatisfied with their appearance."[1] Our discouragement might be related to the fact that the average model weighs 23 percent less than the average woman.[2] The Yale Center calculated how much an average, healthy woman's body would have to change to meet the proportions of the traditional Barbie doll. A woman would need to grow two feet taller, extend her neck length by 3.2 inches, gain 5 inches in chest size, and lose 6 inches in waist circumference.[3]

I think Vickie Heath, First Place 4 Health vice president and author of *Don't Quit, Get Fit*, sums up a better view of beauty: "Strong is the new skinny."[4] Let's focus on wellness, fitness, and health so you can live longer and stronger.

While researching for our book *Red-Hot Monogamy*, we discovered couples that work out together have more sex. There are several reasons for this: 1) Endorphins are released when you exercise, so you are happier, which means you generally like your man better. 2) Exercising together bonds you through a work hard/play hard attitude. 3) When you exercise, you feel better about your body, and that means you will want your husband to see it.

In my book *10 Secrets for Living Smart, Savvy, and Strong*, I (Pam) share details from my personal story of how I lost 50 pounds and have kept it off and regained my health. Here's a *quick list* of how to get healthier:

- ♥ Get a great physician and nutritionist (consult a doctor before you begin any diet or exercise).
- ♥ Get moving (exercise 5 to 6 times a week).
- ♥ Get good nutrition (eat fruits, veggies, and lean protein).
- ♥ Get supplements (vitamins and minerals).
- ♥ Get away from sugar and processed (fast) foods.
- ♥ Get adequate rest (at least 8 hours a night).
- ♥ Get more water and less caffeine.

- ♥ Get a good trainer and some cheerleaders.
- ♥ Get a lifestyle tracker (food and exercise log to track food, sleep, exercise).
- ♥ Picture yourself fit, alive, in love, and beautiful!

When I took steps to regain my health, I felt more confident, sexy, and energetic. We've used our anniversaries to try new activities and buy new fitness gear. We've snowshoed, jet-skiied, cross-country skied, biked, kayaked, and ballroom danced. We've purchased bikes, skates, racquets, and workout gear. For Bill's birthday I gave him a set of 12 red envelopes. Inside each one was a gift card for an "active" date.

Danna Demtre, coauthor of *Lean Body—Fat Wallet,* has seen the positive impact of wellness. "Even after 28 years of marriage...we accept each other's flaws and the normal things that come with aging. But we both appreciate a fit, lean body, and that keeps things *hot* for us!...I think we should give as much attention to pleasing our spouse physically in our later years as we did in our early years!"

Do you not know that you are a temple of God and that the Spirit of God dwells in you? (1 Corinthians 3:16).

♥ Tips for Red-Hot Romance ♥

Which of these activities would your husband like?

- ♥ Take to the dance floor (take line, swing, or ballroom dance classes)

- ♥ Take to the water (kayak, jet ski, water ski, paddleboard, surf, wind surf)

- ♥ Take to the air (parasail, skydive, glider)

- ♥ Take to wheels (bike, motorcycle, skates)

- ♥ Take to ice or snow (ski, snowboard, ice skate, snowshoe, sled)

- ♥ Take up a racquet (tennis, table tennis, badminton, racquetball)

- ♥ Take a swing (baseball, softball, golf)

- ♥ Take a hike (walk; backpack; stroll a lake, park, or beach)

- ♥ Take advantage of technology (Wii fit, Wii dance party)

- ♥ Take up a hunt (camera, rifle, bow and arrow)

- ♥ Take to the gym (cross-fit training, kickbox, Zumba, martial arts)

Try to think of a clever way to invite your guy on one of these active dates: show up in a new workout outfit (or bathing suit); create a clever invitation (tie a hotel key to a golf club), dress up as a hula girl and hold his new surfboard when he enters the house.

> *"For our first anniversary I paid for a scuba class for my husband. Now we've spent years traveling the world to romantic places to dive."*

Becoming a wife who exhibits class, elegance, style; who reflects high standards of personal behavior and is admirably skillful and graceful.

One of my dear friends was sharing how she met her husband at a friend's wedding. Her husband added, "She was so classy!"

I once heard the definition of "good manners" as "the ability to make the people around you feel comfortable about themselves, those around them, and their surroundings." This trait of doing the right thing in the right way at the right time yet not making others feel "less than" is one way to look at classy. A true woman of class knows the traditions of social etiquette and graces. More than this, a true woman of grace and class has the ability to motivate her husband to become a more gallant gentleman. And she does it with love, acceptance, and encouragement.

A classy wife cares more about the people in the room than her entrance into that room. Let's pull out two words that are often coupled with "classy" and wear them like we would a new jacket:

- ♥ *Grace:* the giving of a blessing or favor undeserved.
- ♥ *Mercy:* withholding a penalty or punishment that is deserved.

Do not merely look out for your own personal interests, but also for the interests of others (Philippians 2:4).

♥ Tips for Red-Hot Romance ♥

A classy woman chooses where her mind goes. She selects the thoughts to think about her man. Use this as your filter: "Sisters, whatever is true, whatever is noble, whatever is right, whatever is pure, whatever is lovely, whatever is admirable—if anything is excellent or praiseworthy—think about such things" (Philippians 4:8 NIV).

Protect your love by focusing on what is great about your guy. Using the following list, add a descriptive trait of your husband for each word (for example, for "true" you might write "He keeps his word to me").

My husband is…

- ♥ True:

- ♥ Noble:

- ♥ Right:

- ♥ Pure:

- ♥ Lovely:

- ♥ Admirable:

- ♥ Excellent:

- ♥ Praiseworthy:

Now honor your guy by creating a date that includes some of the finer things in life. On your date share your list with him.

Ritzy. Select a five-star resort and spoil him a little. Have a couple's massage in the spa, lunch by the pool, golf on the executive course, or have appetizers at the top of the hotel. Then hold an "It's all about you—my successful man" celebration behind bedroom doors.

Real. If your husband prefers jeans and boots or shorts and flip-flops, make a five-star dinner and bring the best of life to him. Serve his favorite foods by candlelight in a setting he finds relaxing: the deck, the patio, the barn, the garage, by the fireplace, poolside, on the beach, by a campfire, or under a tree.

"My husband is a 007 fan, so I created 'A License to Thrill' date. I created clues for him that slowly revealed the evening plans and what he needed to do. I rented a sports car for him to drive and dressed up like a 'Bond girl.' He was James Bond for a night!"

Becoming a wife who can show or point out a direction, who makes requests with tactful authority, and who can lay a straight course.

Ask most any husband, and he will say it's sexy when his wife says in bed, "Oh, baby, I love it when you do that!" When we spell out what pleases us in the bedroom, it is a turn-on. How can we carry that sweet side of direction outside the bedroom? There is a fine line between bossy and blessing, and this line is often blurry for wives. It's almost as if bossy is built into our DNA.

When God made Eve, He announced she was "very good." Apparently just by showing up, Eve made life better. When we women have the correct motives, our hearts are pure and we are being led by a heavenly point of view—that's when we're best at helping our husbands, our kids, our churches, and our communities improve. However, many times our motives for helping others are for narcissistic reasons, such as making us look better or getting our way.

By doing a motive check, we can assess if we've crossed that blurry line between bossy and blessing. We sometimes believe in "our better way" so much that we fall into the trap of thinking our ideas are superior to the Creator's. A case in point? God gave Adam and Eve a very clear command to eat from any tree of the garden except one. When the serpent came along, he planted the idea in Eve's mind that God's plan was to clip her wings. Eve, it seems, took a big bite because she thought in doing so she would improve on God's plan (Genesis 3).

The blurry line is the Achilles heel of many women. Once when Maria and her husband, Sam, were team teaching a marriage class, Sam made a comment (perhaps in an attempt at humor) that Maria deemed a bit off. She added in a few words to buffer the situation during the class. After the class, she *continued* her "consulting session" with Sam. "Consulting" is a perfect word to capture the line from "direct" to "diva."

Direct says: I would be so grateful if you would fix the light. You're the best-looking handyman!

Diva says: I've asked you 10 times to fix that light! What's wrong with you? Are you deaf or just lazy?

Direct says: Honey, it would be so incredibly help-ful if we could find some time tonight to discuss our summer vacation.

Diva says: Summer is almost here, and we haven't even discussed what we're going to do for vaca-tion. Do you even have a plan? Do I need to make the decisions, book the tickets, and be our travel agent every vacation?

Direct says: Honey, I'm feeling overwhelmed. I have some ideas on how to get through this intense season. Can we walk the lake path tonight and talk?

Diva says: I got a sitter so let's talk. I wrote up a plan for getting me some help around here. If I waited for you to toss me a life ring, I'd drown.

The temperature of your conversations and your home are influenced by your words. "Be gracious in your speech. The goal is to bring out the best in others in a conversation" (Colossians 4:6).

♥ Tips for Red-Hot Romance ♥

Being direct is an advantage in the bedroom. Try one of these "Baby, I want you" ideas tonight.

♥ Send the kids to Grandpa and Grandma's house. Greet your guy at the door in just an apron, just *his* suit jacket, just a towel…just a "little something." You get the idea.

- ♥ Use rose petals, tea lights, hearts or confetti to create a trail to the bedroom door.

- ♥ Send a "Come home *now,* luv!" text.

- ♥ Slide a hotel key in his pocket or briefcase, tape it to his phone, or put it in the glove box of his vehicle and tape a note to the steering wheel or dash detailing where he should look.

- ♥ Place a sexy item in a gift box and place it where he'll find it quickly when he gets in his vehicle.

Expressive ♥

Becoming a wife who can convey meaning and significance in eloquent, pictorial, vivid, evocative, and flavorful ways.

We have a secret for you, and it's one your husband may not verbalize. For many a man, it is only with his wife that he will share his deepest hopes, fears, frustrations, pains, and stresses. When you are an expressive wife, your husband won't feel so alone in baring his emotions.

Genesis 2:18 notes, "It is not good for the man to be alone." The term "alone" means "to be isolated, curtained off, or in prolonged solitude."

As you express your love to your husband, you create a safe haven for him. Think of it this way. If you were a witness and placed under protection, the authorities would lodge you in a safe house. In the same way, empathy and an expressive, caring heart help create a safe house for your husband. Les and Leslie Parrot, in their book *Trading Places*, recommend a simple empathy process:

> I notice you
> I feel with you, and so
> I act to help you.[1]

One action you can take to help your husband feel safe is to create an "honor journal" to keep your heart soft. Dr. Gary Smalley explains:

> If you want to create a safe environment that encourages healthy relationships to grow, then start by honoring those around you. Picture those individuals as people autographed by God... Imagine giving those people a standing ovation... Another practical way to recognize value...is to keep a list of all the good qualities of that person. I keep several such lists in what I call my Honor Journal. [When I] see them as God sees them... my perspective changes. [2]

Create a personalized journal with a photo of your husband and you on it. Write a list, A to Z, of why you're thankful for your guy. Read it aloud to him.

♥ Tips for Red-Hot Romance ♥

Your husband wants his body touched, but he also wants his heart, mind, and life touched by your care and kindness. Reach out and express your love.

Touch what he loves. If you want to get your man to open up, you need to love what he loves. Hang out side by side doing what he enjoys. Dr. William Harley, in *His Needs, Her Needs,* explains that the number two most pervasive need for a husband is recreational companionship.[3] Mark Driscoll, in *Real Marriage,* advises, "Sometimes it is a great gift to go into your husband's world for a date night by doing something like putting on a jersey, going to a game and eating a hot dog. His love language may just be hot dog." [4] List three or four of your husband's loves. Then ask God to help you show your man that you value what he loves.

Touch his body. You can open your husband emotionally if you touch him physically. We tell couples, "If you give a man your body, he will give you his heart. If you give a woman your heart, she'll give you her body." Sex lowers his stress, but even small physical gestures will lower his tension and entice him to share what is going on in his world. Rub his shoulders, hold his hand, place your arm around him or your hand in his as he is talking, lean on his shoulder and gently rub his chest or walk your fingers across it, give a verbal compliment accompanied by a pat on the back, face him and grab his biceps, walk arm-in-arm, snuggle up close from the back and wrap your arms around his neck or shoulders. When we feel emotionally and physically close, our bodies release oxytocin. "Oxytocin helps ease our fears and increase our trust levels." [5]

Dr. David Schnarch, in his work *Passionate Marriage*, encourages couples to "hug until relaxed." [6] Dr. Gary and Barbara Rosberg suggest sex helps men process life better: "Men often solve problems when they have sex with their wives." [7]

Touch his heart. Listen to your husband. Try the SOFTER listening method:

Stop what you're doing and turn toward your mate.
Open up your body language.
Find key words or a key phrase to repeat.
Try not to take comments personally.
Express affirming emotions.
Respond with loving action.

New York Times bestselling author Stephen Covey states, "Most people do not listen with the intent to understand; they listen with the intent to reply."[8] Listen with your heart. What touch does your man need most today? What will you do to help him?

Fun ♥

Becoming a wife who provides amusement, entertainment, escape, enjoyment, recreation, and laughter; who is playful, delightful, hilarious, and ready for a fling, frolic, romp, spree, merrymaking, or making whoopee.

Comedian Kerri Pomarolli shares how God laid a foundation of fun in her marriage:

> I think it was most evident how much God loved me on the day of our wedding...
>
> It's 1 AM and two overly exhausted people drive back to our hotel giggling like little kids...So we walk upstairs to our hotel room. This would be a change from sharing my bed with Winnie the Pooh.
>
> Something strange and unexpected happened, a

flood of nerves overtook me…I had a loud mouth among my single friends joking about the wild passionate Italian that would finally be unleashed and I didn't feel wild at all…We open the door to the room and I couldn't believe the sight before me. The room was flooded with rose petals and candles. A warm bath was drawn and filled with rose petals…It was more romantic than I could have ever dreamed…

I had spent many hours preparing and dreaming of the perfect, exquisite, beautiful outfit to wear on this special night. I was quite pleased with my choice…[of] a shimmering white silk nightgown with tiny beaded straps and I knew it would be just right. Ron decided to retire to the bathroom to "slip into something more comfortable"…

As I waited to see what sexy and thoughtful outfit my new groom had selected, I quickly slipped into my gown and took my place lounging on our rose-covered bed. As the minutes ticked by I practiced different poses trying to emulate all the…model poses I had seen…I tried some of their "sexy" lounging positions and I looked like I was in a bad game of Twister!

Finally the door opened and before my eyes appeared my husband smiling…in his favorite flannel bright yellow plaid sweatpants and an oversized T-shirt with a huge rubber ducky cartoon with the words "Don't Worry, Be Happy." He took one look at me, and then glanced down at himself, and in his own charming way just uttered, "Uh oh!" and started humming "Do doo doo doo, doo doo doo doo…Don't worry, be happy now!" And that's exactly what I did!

A cheerful heart is good medicine (Proverbs 17:22 NIV).

Bill says, "Sometimes we have sex and think, 'Wow! Life just can't get better than this!' Sometimes we have a sexual encounter with our spouse and think, 'Hmm, that was awkward.'" Keep laughing and enjoying each other.

♥ Tips for Red-Hot Romance ♥

In *Kiss Me Like You Mean It,* author Dave Clarke encourages, "The activity alone should never be the focus. The focus is unpredictable fun, laughter, chemistry, intimacy and sexual desire you create during the activity…Love is fun. Love is a blast."[1] On your wedding day, perhaps you had "something old, something new, something borrowed, and something blue." Shift that thinking over to your romantic life.

♥ *Something old.* "My husband and I wrote our names and wedding date with permanent marker on different rocks. We hid them in special places of ours, and then we drew a treasure map. We have since moved, so we plan a trip down memory lane to go back and see how many we can find.

"We try to locate a heart shaped rock from each place we travel. We have a jar on our night-stand and each one reminds us of a happy day in our life." (Idea: Learn to give a hot stone massage.)

♥ *Something new.* Here's an old excuse used in a new and better way, thanks to the creativity of the author of *Generation NeXt Marriage* Tricia Goyer. "Fake a headache…for my husband's sake. Since we have older kids, it goes something like this: 'It's been a long day. I'm wiped out. I think Daddy and I are heading to bed.'"

♥ *Something borrowed.* Sheila Gregoire, in *Good Girls Guide to Great Sex*, gives a new twist to familiar fortune cookies. Read the fortune but add an "in bed" tacked on to what the fortune reads. Here are a few that tickled our funny bone:

- ♥ You will receive many praises and acknowledgements from your hard work in bed.

- ♥ You are efficient and can easily adapt to different environments in bed.

- ♥ Something unusual is going to happen to you at work or school or in bed.

♥ *Something blue.* Skip the blue and jump to red. Men find women sexier and more attractive when wearing red. Your husband will be more likely to want to have sex and spend money on you when you're wearing red.[2] So get a new, sexy, red nightie, tank top, or bathing suit. Consider wearing red every day!

Becoming a wife of favorable character: suitable, honorable, wholesome, competent, credible, commendable, well-grounded, wise, possessing common sense.

"Good" in Sanskrit is *gadhya*, meaning "what one clings to."[1] When a man finds a good woman, he wants to cling to her and hopes and prays she clings to him.

Proverbs 18:22 asserts, "He who finds a wife finds a good thing and obtains favor [approval and delight] from the LORD." The goodness of a man having a wife is captured in the story of creation. After creating Adam, God said, "It is *not good* for the man to be alone" (Genesis 2:18). Then God created Eve as a helper suitable for Adam. After creating Adam and Eve, "God saw all that He had made, and behold, it was very good" (Genesis 1:31). The word translated "good" in this verse is the Hebrew word *tôb*, which means "beautiful or functioning the way God intended." When we wives are functioning as we were created: balanced, whole, healthy in all the major areas of life, we help our husbands and our families live congruently and intentionally too.

Think of life like a wheel on a bicycle. Each spoke helps hold the tire in place so it rolls smoothly. But if a few spokes break, the wheel flattens and eventually the tire will not roll. For instance, we know more than one couple where the lack of housekeeping skills contributed to the end of their marriages. It's hard to make love in a bed if it can't be located! Small things do matter. Why not interview your mate? Ask him, "What is one thing I can do that you believe would make the most positive difference in our life together and marriage?"

Sources of tension in my marriage to Bill have been my lack of culinary interest and my spontaneous attitude toward spending money. When Bill and

I brainstormed about my forgetting to record in the register what I was spending, a simple solution ended our arguments. He ordered checks with duplicate slips.

As for cooking, when our sons were small, Bill and I went to Hawaii for our 15-year anniversary. Our eldest son, a middle-schooler at the time, raved on and on about his aunt's cooking. My sister-in-law said, "It can't be that much better than your mom makes at home." Our son replied, "If it doesn't involve a box and a microwave, it doesn't happen at our house." That comment was a motivation changer! I have a long way to go, but Bill is enjoying my inner chef being released.

Bill's weakness is being so people oriented that he never checks his watch when talking or listening so he runs late. Now he stops by the flowershop and comes home with a beautiful but inexpensive bouquet. He figures the flowers will buy him grace with me. It does!

It is vital to take an honest look at our weaknesses and seek to shore them up. When we offer to make a change, our spouses might offer to make some improvements too. One wife shared this fun example:

> We had recently moved and needed to move some boxes into the basement. The kids had already been put to bed, so to make it more fun and give my husband incentive to do it quickly...for every trip we made I "lost" a piece of clothing. I have

never seen him move boxes so quickly! Of course, "horizontal fellowship" followed!

Ask, "Honey, what *one goal* in each area of our life together would you recommend I work toward for the next year?

- ♥ Physically:

- ♥ Relationally:

- ♥ Financially:

- ♥ Vocationally:

- ♥ Sexually:

- ♥ Domestically:

Which do you prefer I begin with?

Which area do you think is my strongest?

Don't be afraid of this discussion with your mate. Dr. John Gottman discovered that couples who had the most passion in their sex lives were also the most volatile outside the bedroom.[2] "They express more negative *and* more positive emotions."[3]

♥ Tips for Red-Hot Romance ♥

Here are a few ideas to link each area of your life together to the bedroom.

Domestically. Spruce up your bedroom. Get some new sheets. (To explore your romantic decorating style, see our book *Red-Hot Monogamy*.) Put some creativity and energy into keeping your bedroom a sanctuary of love.

Financially. Give your husband his own personal "dollar dance."

Physically. Take him to your favorite sports store. Try on outfits and purchase the ones that are *his* favorite. When you're home, ask him to undress his favorite athlete—you! One wife shared, "My man loves biking, so I planned a bike trip between bed and breakfast hotels."

Relationally. Have a trophy, T-shirt, or fake magazine cover made that extols your husband as "The World's Best…" (you fill in the blank).

Sexually. Using a regular deck of cards, play "Slap Jack." Anytime a face card shows up, whoever slaps the discard pile first decides who has to take off a piece of clothing.

Vocationally. Slide a love note in his sack lunch that invites him to join you in "the sack" after work.

Humble ♥

> *Becoming a wife who is not proud, haughty, or arrogant; who is unpretentious, demure, down-to-earth, modest, unassuming.*

When we turn our eyes and energies toward others—that's the key to humility.

> *With the humble is wisdom* (Proverbs 11:2).
>
> *A humble spirit will obtain honor* (29:23).

Those who humble themselves will be exalted (Luke 14:11 NIV).

A wife who sees herself accurately doesn't need to be the center of attention all the time. When we are not "all about us," we gain the ability to be more about our men. In an interview, psychologist Juli Slattery, author of *Finding the Hero in Your Husband*, shared:

> God created man in such a way that he really needs a good woman to bring out that hero in him. God has equipped a woman with the skills... to help her husband develop into a strong leader. [1]

❧ Tips for Red-Hot Romance ❧

Bring out the hero in your husband!

Satisfy him sexually. Dr. Kevin Leman wrote, "A sexually fulfilled husband will feel good about himself. So much of who we are as men is tied into how our wives respond to us sexually...[Every] healthy man wants to be his wife's hero." [2] If your husband is sexually fulfilled, he'll do anything for you. Satisfying your man, motivates your man.

Speak his value. Your words are the "Shazam!" that transforms an ordinary man into Captain Marvel. My nickname for Bill is Superman, so I asked him one day,

"What makes you feel like a hero?" Bill answered, "Pam, when I hear you brag 'My husband can fix anything,' 'My husband is my hero,' or 'I can't make my life work without my Bill,' it makes me feel great."

Share his load. In response to what makes him feel heroic, Bill also added, "And I love it when you laugh at my jokes." When you flirt with your hero—giggling at his attempts at levity, when you give him a sensual hug when he is covered with sweat from some back-breaking job, when you give him a luscious kiss even when he is covered head to toe with dirt, when the grease under his fingernails is an aphrodisiac so you tear off his clothes and join him in the shower…he will live to be your hero yet another day!

Interesting ♥

Becoming a wife who can hold your husband's attention because you are amazing, astonishing, breathtaking, captivating, engaging, enthralling, exciting, exhilarating, fascinating, intriguing, stimulating, thrilling, and surprising.

One of our audience members shared this creative memory with us:

> One Valentine's Day I left a card on the counter so my husband would see it at noon. It told him to be at a certain address by 4 PM, and to bring a suit to put on later. When he arrived, he discovered it was an appointment for a massage. Afterward, he changed into the dress clothes he'd brought. I then sent him a text with the next address of where he was to go. The greeter at the front desk informed him that there was a hot blond waiting for him. In the room I was sitting there all decked out. I bought his dinner. He loved the mystery adventure!

> *May your fountain be blessed, and may you rejoice in the wife of your youth...May her breasts satisfy you always, may you ever be intoxicated with her love* (Proverbs 5:18-19 NIV).

Mystery! Intrigue! Dave Clark, an award-winning songwriter and speaker on creativity, wrote:

> Sometimes romance is more about being willing to break some patterns. I'm always looking for new ways to drive against the flow of traffic. One thing that comes to mind that is always fun is to

dress up in fancy clothes and map out a progressive dinner of fast-food restaurants (salad at Arby's, McDonald's for fries, Wendy's for a chicken sandwich). It's not about the food; the romance is in the *adventure*. (The fancy clothes are to make people wonder what you're up to.)

Take the simple and turn it into a *"Wow!"*

♥ Tips for Red-Hot Romance ♥

Sexy dates don't have to be a drain on the family budget. (At our website www.Love-Wise.com you'll find an article called "Recession Romance" that includes romance ideas that are either free or almost free.) Dr. Douglas Rosenau says, "Sex is 80% imagination and mind and 20% friction."[1] Here are some homemade romance ideas.

It's not a walk-in closet—it's the inside of a Bedouin tent. Using sheets and Christmas lights, line the inside of your closet. Throw down sofa cushions and pillows to create your Bedouin love nest. After that, every time your husband opens the closet he will think of *you!*

It's not a garden hose—it's your outdoor shower. Send the kids to the grandparents', put up some sheets or move those ficus trees into a screening circle, and together enjoy your backyard "waterfall."

It's not a shower stall—it's a photo booth. Take some fun props into your "booth" and snap some kissing pictures. Props can be a boa, beads, hats, and sunglasses. Keep the pictures PG-rated in case the kids pick up your camera.

It's not a dining room—it's a five-star restaurant. Cook at home but wow it up by using white linens, candles, and music. Afterward, clear the dishes and make love on the table. (You'll see him smile during family dinners for a while!)

It's not the backyard—it's a mountain camping spot. Pop up the tent, throw in *one* sleeping bag, and snuggle.

It's not a piano—it's a sultry seat. Perch yourself seductively in a red dress and serenade your man. That flat surface can create your own music.

It's not a backyard charcoal grill—it's a romantic fire pit. Drop the legs of the barbecue and toast up S'mores while you kiss beside the glowing embers.

It's not a garage—it's a drive-in movie. Climb into the backseat, put your laptop on the dash, play a romantic movie and steam up those windows.

It's not the patio—it's the deck of a cruise ship. Wrap the awning poles in lights, light tiki torches, and float candles in the pool (even a kiddie pool). Dance the night away.

> "My in-laws were visiting for three weeks. Even though they're wonderful, by the end of two weeks my husband and I were craving alone time. I said, 'Honey, why don't you take me to work today. When you pick me up, we can go "parking" before we go home.' (I got off work at 9 PM, the kids were already in bed, and we own 20 acres around our home.) We both had something to look forward to all day, and we enjoyed that night!"

Becoming a wife who promotes happiness, bliss, and delight because she is rosy, glad, pleased, satisfied, tickled, cheerful, lighthearted, sunny, upbeat, elated, euphoric, exhilarated, exuberant, jubilant, and thrilled.

Are you full of positive emotion? According to the documentary *Happy*, we all have a happiness set point in our DNA. [1] On a scale of 1 to 100, this happiness set point accounts for about 50 percent of how happy we are. Things often associated with the pursuit of happiness: money, status, and success account for about

10 percent, so the other 40 percent are activities and choices we make.

A few undertakings that plant happiness seeds include physical activities that release dopamine (aerobic exercise is one of the best sources), variety (doing things just a little differently, traveling to different places, meeting new people, reading new books; for red-hot romance this can include changing the place, position, or priority of sex), and flow (having meaningful and enjoyable work or activities so we lose track of time). Other happiness sparks include a strong relationship system, personal growth, giving to others, and counting blessings daily.

If you're happy, it will be easier for your husband to be happy. *Joy is a choice.* Before one particularly challenging time in our life together, our marriage was strong, our kids were making wise choices, and we had gained a measure of success. Then the attacks came. Bill didn't feel well. His blood pressure was erratically high. He was in pain, and he struggled to concentrate. All this got his attention because his father had a stroke leaving him disabled and Bill's grandfather died of a stroke in his forties. Bill eventually resigned his pastorate, and we focused solely on writing and speaking. The transition was difficult on many levels. I'd never seen my husband so discouraged. I knew God was calling me to "carry" Bill's heart.

I set aside extra time to listen to Bill process his feelings. I found Scripture verses to encourage him and prayed those verses over him. I looked for opportunities for him to connect with friends and favorite activities. We released endorphins through humor and exercise. We continued to help others with their relationships because Bill feels stronger helping others. I printed out verses of God's favor, goodness, and joy. I hung my heart and mind on God's wisdom.

If people asked "How are you?" my answer was "Choosin' joy!" because "the joy of the LORD is [my] strength" (Nehemiah 8:10). God empowered me so I could empower my husband. Daily I asked the family, "Who got a postcard of God's love?" We went on joy hunts—and we found it! Bill and I grew closer, stronger, and more intimate.

Three principles I prayed for Bill constantly were drawn from the book of Job: "The LORD restored the fortunes...the LORD increased all that Job had two-fold...the LORD blessed the latter days of Job more than his beginning" (Job 42:10,12). I prayed that God would double the length of Bill's life and influence.

Sometimes we wives are fearful when our husbands have a health scare. Ed Wheat, MD, in *Intended for Pleasure*, explains that a man is ready for sex physically if he can climb a flight of stairs, walk briskly for two blocks, or drive in traffic.[2] Bill could do all those things, so red-hot monogamy became a shelter from the storm. Together we focused on what we had, not on what we'd lost. We looked to the future blessings.

God has more than doubled His blessings on us! Bill's health is completely restored. He speaks to audiences worldwide, has penned many books, and has enjoyed wonderful times with our children, their spouses, and our grandchildren, who all adore their happy "Papa."

♥ Tips for Red-Hot Romance ♥

"I can out joke you" walk. We would walk and quote one-liners, tossing puns back and forth and quote motivational sayings or encouraging verses.

Melodrama date. The slapstick humor helped us laugh away our troubles.

"Third base." We'd recite old radio or TV classic comedy routines like "Who's on first?" and listen to clean comedy radio.

Night at the Improv. We loved attending clean, improvisational comedy performances, but funds were tight so we made our own sexual improv. Each partner takes a paper bag, sets a timer for five minutes, and then runs through the house or garage gathering odd, wild, weird, obscure items. Then we meet back in the bedroom, trade bags, and see who can come up with the most creative ways to use the items as foreplay.

Child's play. Have squirt gun or water balloons fights, tickle matches, jump on the trampoline (or bed), use the swings at a playground, splash in the pool, or do the Twist.

Becoming a wife who is friendly, generous, sympathetic, understanding; charitable, humane, considerate, forbearing, tolerant, agreeable, affectionate, and gentle.

Sharon Jaynes, author of *Become the Woman of His Dreams*, shared how she encourages romance:

When I walk through the den with fresh sheets, or if Steve is helping me put them on the bed, I suggest we try them out to see if they still work.

One weekend when I was away, I put red heart stickers in strategic places for Steve to find (in his underwear drawer, on his toothbrush handle, on his pillow, on his steering wheel). He called and let me know each time he found one.

One Valentine's Day I made a heart-shaped yard sign that said "Sharon loves Steve!" I placed it outside the window at his dental office.

Be kind! It's so easy to fall into a negative downward spiral. Remember, *you chose him,* so disparaging him is calling yourself unwise. Allow love to change *you* into a kind woman with positive words.

If you catch your mind wanting to slip into sarcasm, stop and choose to say just the opposite of what you were feeling or about to say. For example, if you were thinking...

- ♥ "You are so stupid," say instead, "You come up with the most clever ideas!"

- ♥ "You fool," say instead, "I know you will make the wise choice."

- ♥ "Are you kidding!" say instead, "Tell me more about that idea."

- ♥ "What!" say instead, "I'd love to hear your thoughts on that."

Get it? In your mind tell yourself, *Stop! What is the opposite of this negative thought? How can I change it into a positive?* And then do it.

Catch your man off guard with your kindness. John and Anita Renfroe capture this type of kindness in their devotional for couples *Duets: Still in the Word...Still in the Mood*:

> O my dove, [while you are here] in the seclusion of the clefts in the solid rock, in the sheltered and secret place of the cliff, let me see your face... your face is lovely (Songs of Songs 2:14 AMP).
>
> Behold the power of the tryst. (Doesn't it just sound sexy?) There is no denying that this couple knew how to keep the love hot and happening. They would slip away into the "seclusion of the clefts"...nothing makes you feel more dangerous than when you are taking love when it is unexpected...wouldn't it just jump up anticipation in your relationship if both of you agreed to plan some sort of surprise tryst with each other?...Prepare for some exciting, secretive love! [1]

Express your kindness by passing a secret message to your spouse inviting him for a tryst. Slide a note into his suit pocket with a secret rendezvous point, whisper the invitation to him during a meeting, or text him a message that only he will understand. Plan a special expression of appreciation for him when he arrives at the designated secluded place.

❧ Tips for Red-Hot Romance ❧

"Let us show gratitude" (Hebrews 12:28).

The word "gratitude" means "an expression of thankfulness." Select one way to say, "Thank you!"

- ♥ Post-it note his car with hundreds of colorful sticky notes that say "Thank you!"
- ♥ Put his favorite home-baked goodie on his desk with a thank-you note.
- ♥ Write "Thank you, husband!" in colored chalk on the driveway.
- ♥ Write "Thank you for being *you*!" on his window sunshield.
- ♥ Etch "Thank you, my love!" in the steam on the mirror while he takes a shower.
- ♥ Spray paint a sheet with "Thank you, honey!" and hang it on a balcony, deck, or clothesline.
- ♥ Text "Thx 4 being U" to his cell phone.
- ♥ Make a paper chain of all the reasons you're thankful for him. Hang it over his mirror, headboard, or on the bedroom wall.
- ♥ Create a thank-you card online and email it to your man.

"Beginning on Feb. 1 and continuing every day for 14 days, I made a little heart, wrote something I admired about my husband on it, and gave it to him."

"My husband came home one day to a treasure hunt of rose petals and love notes that ended at the bathroom mirror, which was covered in Post-it Notes of love."

Loving ♥

Becoming a wife who is affectionate, adoring, devoted, caring, compassionate, considerate, forgiving, understanding, warm, amorous, and sentimental.

Dr. Kevin Leman, in his book *Sheet Music*, wrote, "More important than your breast size, more important than your waist size, more important than the length of your legs is your attitude. The vast majority of men would rather have a wife who is a little on the plain side but has a sexually available attitude than a drop-dead gorgeous woman who treats her husband like ice…" [1]

When wives lack the desire to wow their husbands, I encourage them to pray, "Lord, give me the 'want to' to even want to wow my man." Gary and Barbara Rosberg, in *The 5 Sex Needs of Men and Women*, reveal that nearly 61 percent of men share that their wives' sexual initiation is a top sexual need. "When a wife...pursues [her man] sexually, he feels on top of the world."[2]

♥ Tips for Red-Hot Romance ♥

Work on cultivating an "I am available" attitude. Arlene Pellicane in her book *31 Days to a Happy Husband,* dares women to take a month and focus on their husbands. She shares how a simple trip to a market highlighted a need many wives find common:

> One day we walked up to the meat counter... Looking up we saw the big electronic number that showed who was being served. We looked for the machine and found it. It read, "Take a number."
>
> I wonder if your husband ever feels that way.
>
> Forget having sex. The kids are up with runny noses.
>
> *Take a number.*
>
> Can we reschedule our breakfast date? Mary called me for coffee...
>
> *Take a number.*
>
> The women's ministry team needs me to create centerpieces...
>
> *Take a number.* [3]

The average for couples to have coitus used to be two or three times a week; the frequency is declining to a little more often than once a week.[4] A wife in one of our audiences shared, "If you asked my husband, he would tell you that the most romantic thing I ever did for him was to give him the gift of two weeks of sex as often as he wanted with no excuses from me. He said later it really wasn't the sex that was the best part (although he *really* enjoyed it!), but it was the fact that I was willing to sacrifice something to...meet his needs." Select one of these spicy sex challenges to initiate.

100 hot days. Gary Stollman, a relationship expert said, "One hundred days of straight sex is not necessarily going to fix things, but it is a great metaphor for putting the energy back into a relationship." [5]

60 days or 7 days. Tony and Alisa DiLorenzo write in their book *7 Days of Sex Challenge*, "Eleven years into our marriage we were at a crossroads...We were present but not actively growing closer...[so] we did something completely out of our comfort zone. We decided to challenge ourselves to 60 Days of Sex!...We needed to break out of the rut we had been in." [6] Since that first challenge, they have scaled it down to a 7-day challenge, and they have completed that four times.

10 percent more. Dr. Gary and Barbara Rosberg suggest

an incremental change: "Wives, what would happen if you responded sexually to your husband 10 percent more than you do now?" [7]

TV-less dare. TV in the bedroom steals intimacy. Instead go to bed and read a chapter of Song of Solomon together.

Wow! Plan ahead. Our book *Red-Hot Monogamy* is an *8-week guide* to turning up the heat behind your bedroom door (or other places). My (Pam) book *52 Ways to Wow Your Husband* provides suggestions for romancing your husband for a full year.

Sheila Wray Gregoire, author of *The Good Girl's Guide to Great Sex*, initiates a "29 Days to Great Sex Challenge": "Each day will have a little exercise you can do to make your sex life wonderful—or to just get you going in the right direction." [8]

Moral ♥

Becoming a wife who is ethical, knows principles of right and wrong, operates from her conscience, and is decent, honest, righteous, upright, virtuous, and noble.

Most of you own GPS devices. The path of love can be simplified by using "GPS questions." Before Bill or I say or do anything, we ask, "Does this show love for...

God?
People?
Self?

Implementing this GPS guide can help you navigate moral love choices. Fidelity is the trait that most secures your love. By keeping your vows, you produce a trusted, red-hot love environment. The most asked question Bill and I get when it comes to red-hot sex is, "What is okay with God?" Our answer? You can say *yes* if you:

Yield to one another. Everything done is agreed upon by both parties. "Over all these virtues put on love, which binds them all together in perfect unity" (Colossians 3:14 NIV).

Extend it in love. No one should feel forced or coerced. Sex should reflect love and never demean or inflict pain. Sex is a relationship to protect. "Marriage must be respected by all, and the marriage bed kept undefiled" (Hebrews 13:4 HCSB).

Secure it with privacy. Sex should only be you two alone. No other partners, no pornography, no fake imitations of body parts. When it comes to gray areas or things not specifically forbidden, apply this wisdom: "Everything is permissible (allowable and lawful) for me; but not all things are helpful (good for me to do, expedient and profitable when considered with other things). Everything is lawful for me, but I will not become the slave of anything or be brought under its power" (1 Corinthians 6:12 AMP).

God gives us elbow room to make choices, but never risk your partner's or your life, health, and reputation for a few moments of ecstasy. (At www.Love-Wise.com, we offer an article called "What's Okay with God in the Bedroom?" that discusses gray areas and common questions.)

As a gift to your husband, clear your schedule, put on some romantic music, and then touch, caress, compliment, and kiss your nude husband head to toe. Or take turns! Read the passages and follow the king and his wife's blueprint for love. (See Song of Songs 4:1-7; 5:1-16; 7:1-10 for inspiration.)

Take time to kneel and pray at the foot of your marriage bed and claim your love as a reflection of God's love. As a token of fidelity, select a scent or fragrance that symbolizes purity to both of you (lily, rose, mint) and spray the sheets with it. Men appear to be

turned on most by a combination of smelling laven-
der and pumpkin pie; women by licorice and cucum-
ber.[1] Smells that remind guys of a happy childhood win
points too (think cookies or banana bread).[2] Another
option is scented candles. Men's favorite scents appear
to be vanilla, musk, ginger, peppermint, Ylang Ylang,
and nutmeg.[3] Whenever and wherever you happen to
smell your choice of fragrance, you will be reminded of
the pleasure of committed, marital love.

♥ Tips for Red-Hot Romance ♥

Think about your husband's sex drive as a gift. Men's
sex drive is strongest under age 30; women's is stronger from ages 30 to 50. In years to come, it might be
you who wants sex more than he does. When that time
comes, you'll be glad you said "Yes!" to him now. Here
are some fun ways to say yes today.

- ♥ Write "Yes!" on the sidewalk to your front door.

- ♥ Write "Yes!" on a poster and hang it on the
  garage door.

- ♥ Write "Yes!" through the steam on the mirror.

- ♥ Write "Yes!" in lipstick and seal it with a lipstick kiss on the rearview mirror of his car.

- ♥ Write "Yes!" and text it with a *tasteful* photo.
  Remember, digital is forever.

- ♥ Call and say, "Yes! Yes! Yes! *Oh yes!* I'm so looking forward to spending time with you tonight!"
- ♥ Make a series of "Yes!" sticky notes (in bright pink or cut in heart shapes) and place them in random places along a path he'll walk.

Nurturing ♥

Becoming a wife who knows how to equip, nourish, foster, cultivate, promote, champion, support, boost, and uphold the best for her husband.

Often when I speak for a "Wow Wife" night, I share a story about a friend who spoke to my mentor, Sally Conway, about her mid-life marriage. Sally wisely said, "Look at your husband through the eyes of a younger woman. What traits, what attributes, what qualities would a younger woman find attractive? Go and find those things attractive too. Your husband doesn't need a mother. He needs a girlfriend." Shortly after one of those "Wow Wife" nights, I received this email:

Did you know if you spell *wow* backward you still

get *wow*? If you hold *wow* up to the mirror you still read *wow*? If you read *wow* upside down you get *mom*? Don't do that! Your husband doesn't need a *mom*; he needs a *wow wife*.

My friend Jill Savage encourages moms who attend Hearts at Home events: "Wife, first; Mom, second." It's so easy to drift to the mommy side of the street once kids have entered the picture. For example, while writing this book our DVR system got a glitch, and Bill is always the hero who fixes it. One night I shared at dinner that it was acting up again. Bill said, "So, are you asking me to fix it now or just informing me?" I replied curtly, "I just said it wasn't working" (in a motherly "if I've told you once, I've told you a thousand times" tone). Instead, I should have said with a smile, "That would be amazing if you could fix it now. You're always my hero." "Wives, understand and support your husbands in ways that show your support for Christ" (Ephesians 5:22 MSG).

There's a joke that expresses this womanly dilemma of balancing wife vs. mom: "One of our presidents was walking with his wife, who sees one of her old boyfriends in a less-than-glorious occupation. The president remarks, "If you hadn't married me, you might be married to that guy." The first lady answers calmly, "If I had married him, he'd be president."

How can you nurture your husband as his wife rather than as his mom?

A wife flirts. She has full confidence in his success.
A mom fine-tunes. She is fearful he might fail.

A wife asks. "What would you like me to do to help?"
A mom commands. "This is what needs to be done."

A wife releases. She trusts things will be right.
A mom hovers. She worries things will not be right.

Marcia Ramsland, the "Organizing Pro" and author of *Simplify Your Life*, helps us recognize when we've crossed over the double-yellow line between wife and mom: "I simplify David's life by telling him 'reminders'…One morning when he was walking out the door for work, I spouted off three 'reminders'…He said, 'You're on my runway.' I immediately became aware that this wasn't the best time to talk to him."

♥ Tips for Red-Hot Romance ♥

Get off your husband's runway so your love is cleared for takeoff.

Carefree camping. A sweet woman pulled me aside and told me her story of going on a cross-country trip in a pop up camper. Since the little ones were along the couple had weeks of closeness but no sex. They were desperate, so in the middle of the night, as silently as possible, they made love. Right as they came to climax and could use some audio camouflage, a train roared by with a loud "Whoo whoot!" From then on their code word for desiring sex was "I think I hear the train."

Comical code. Use a funny memory to create your own code. One family played the "dog pile" game except they called it hamburger, meaning one person is the bun, another a patty, another a tomato slice, another an onion, and so forth. One day after church my friend and her husband were in their room changing clothes and one thing led to another. They slid between the sheets only to have their grade-schooler barge in, see them snuggling, and shout to his siblings, "Hey, Mom and Dad are playing hamburger!" All the kids ran to the bedroom to join the fun. Trying to maintain their composure, the couple told the children to leave. When they were gone, the couple locked the door. Since that day, if one of them is interested in sex, they ask, "Want hamburgers tonight?"

Flirty fast car. An attendee at one of our marriage conferences rented a sports car to get to the conference with her husband. Even though the kids were along, her man felt he was being romanced because she'd arranged for him to drive the car of his dreams.

Optimistic ♥

Becoming a wife who anticipates favorable outcomes and is hopeful, confident, assured, idealistic, perky, and maintains an uplifting viewpoint.

There is a story of a married man who went out with friends and arrived home late. He was hoping for a little "red-hot monogamy," but when he arrived home he found his wife snoring away. He went and got a bottle of aspirin and dropped two into her mouth. She promptly woke up choking. "What are you doing?" she asked.

He replied, "I thought you needed a couple aspirin."

"No! I don't have a headache!"

"That's all I wanted to hear!"[1]

That man was optimistic! I (Pam) remember praying about this verse regarding marriage and sex in 1 Corinthians 7:5: "Stop depriving one another." My prayer went something like this:

> *Lord, You know I absolutely love sex with Bill. But You also know I struggle with migraines. I want to say "yes" to Bill as much as possible, but I get these headaches so I can legitimately say, "Not tonight, dear. I have a headache." Help!*

Later I was sitting in my doctor's office reading an article that said sex opens up the blood vessels, which would lessen migraine pain. Now I say, "Yes, tonight. I have a headache!"

♥ Tips for Red-Hot Romance ♥

Give your husband hope by creating new roles for yourself.

Fan club president. Mail a fan letter to your husband from "the president of your Fan Club" and invite him to a fan club meeting. Do a "fan dance," using the fans seductively to cover key parts of your nude body.

Biz manager. A business manager looks over the wellness of a company. Joe and Michelle, authors of *Yes! Your Marriage Can Be Saved* and *Marriage 911*, had a history of multiple divorces before they came to know God personally. They determined that their marriage was going to last!

> Joe and I had a big issue resurface that we thought was forever gone. After a couple of days of prayer, making some important changes in our life, and working through the forgiveness stage, we decided to go on a "honeymoon" to recapture the intimacy…We made our reservations a week ahead at a quaint romantic hotel. The week leading up to our getaway was filled with flirting, love notes,

teasing, and the anticipation of intimately reconnecting. We consider it one of the most romantic times in our marriage.

Time keeper. In our book *Red-Hot Monogamy,* we present an acrostic for how much TIME it takes to have a red-hot relationship.

Take 10 to 20 minutes a day for "chat time" to touch base emotionally

Invest in a weekly date night (at home or on the town)

Monthly day off to do any activity *together* for at least 6 hours

Escape once a year for a marriage conference to gain skills *and* once a year to rest and recharge.

Growing old together requires a good sense of humor, especially with the evidence of hearing loss. One of our friends shared this story with us.

My husband and I are in our late 50s, but we still enjoy a fun and flirtatious relationship. Naturally, I was intrigued one day when in the middle of a discussion about our retirement property I heard him say, "By the way, we're going to have lots of morning sex up there."

Once I heard that, it was all I could think about.

My imagination ran wild, and I wondered why our physical relationship would be so special up there.

I smiled playfully and watched with amusement as my man went on and on about the building project.

Finally he stopped and asked me what I was smiling at.

I replied, "We're going to have lots of morning sex up there, huh? I'm anxious to hear why it will be so extraordinary!"

He stared at me with a confused expression for a moment. Then his look softened and he smiled at me. He kindly stated, "Sweetheart, I said there will be 'a lot more insects up there.'"

Passionate ♥

Becoming a wife who is enthusiastic, aroused, excited, blazing, and demonstrative.

You can *choose* to fan the flame of your passion. Even if you only have a small ember of love, with a little tender-loving attention you can grow that glow so your love will reappear fiery hot. Jay and Laura Laffoon, authors of *He Said. She Said.*, share their secret to creating a bonfire of love. Jay tells this story:

Our friends Stacey and Dottie Foster live in Detroit and pastor Life Changers International... I was with the Fosters on a mission trip...After a day of touring the Compassion projects, Stacey, Dottie, and I had dinner...As the conversation turned toward *Celebrate Your Marriage* and the couples we were working with, we began to talk about the common challenges couples face. Naturally one of those common challenges is sex.

Dottie said, "Men need to understand that, for women, there are four weeks in every month." All of a sudden I was a bit confused and wondered, *Aren't there four weeks in every month for a man too?* At this point Dottie made herself perfectly clear. She elaborated, "Because of the hormonal changes in a woman, each one of the four weeks has its own distinct personality:

Week one: I think my husband is a pretty good guy. I think he's a good father and a good provider. I'm proud to call him my husband. I like him, but that's about it.

Week two: I can't keep my hands off my husband. I think he's the most wonderful man on the planet and I can't get enough of him. He just drives me crazy (in a good way). All I want to do is be "with" him.

Week three: I can't stand my husband, or any man on the planet for that matter. He just drives me crazy (in a bad way).

Week four: I feel like my husband is my buddy. Because of my monthly visitor, we're just roommates."

The lightbulb went on in my head. Instantly I replayed the years of our marriage and could identify this exact pattern. [1]

So Jay and Laura created a plan that helps a couple maximize passion based on this "natural rhythm."

14 Days a Year to a Better Marriage

♥ 15 minutes per day of conversation (15 minutes x 365 = 4 days a year)

♥ 1 hour a week together (1 hour x 365 = 2 days a year)

♥ 4 hour date night per month (4 hours x 12 = 2 days a year)

♥ 2 day getaway twice a year (2 days x 2 = 4 days)

♥ 25 minutes of sex every 3 days (or the average of every three days based upon the rhythm above) = 2 days a year.

All this equals 14 days! In just 14 days you can have a more passionate marriage!

Your passion for your husband is good for his health too. Mehmet Oz, MD, shared a study that concluded that men who ejaculated between 13 and 20 times a month decreased their risk of prostate cancer by 14 percent, and men who ejaculated more than 21 times a month decreased it by 43 percent. [2]

Many waters cannot quench love (Song of Solomon 8:7).

∾ Tips for Red-Hot Romance ∾

Special calendars. Give your husband a calendar with hearts placed on each red-hot monogamy day. (You can also mark the calendars to reflect the rhythm the Laffoons laid out.)

The ultimate coupon. Give your husband a set of coupons for "sex when *he* wants it." You can give 14 coupons as a symbol of 14 days to a more passionate love. Or give him enough coupons for sex three days a week (121 times per year).

Bonus intimacy. Fill a crystal bowl with however many heart-shaped gems or tokens you're willing to give him for "spontaneous red-hot romance" outside your normal routine. To redeem a token, he simply needs to place one on your nightstand to let you know he desires you sexually.

> *"To keep the spark in my marriage, I randomly put sticky notes on something for my husband to see that reads, 'Turn me on instead' (on a lamp, his iPhone, his iPad, shower head, etc.)."*

Quiet Spirit ♥

Becoming a wife who is calm, gentle, easygoing, peaceful, relaxed, still, serene, and tranquil.

Speaking at our friend Carol Garlow's funeral were leading politicians, pastors of mega churches and mega ministries, TV personalities, and renowned journalists. They were drawn to pay tribute, as we were, because of Carol's quiet, powerful, inner strength and her steadfast love for her husband, Jim. We watched Carol during her long battle with cancer stand strong next to her husband. Her consistent love and diligent prayers for her man fueled his ability to lead a church and talk to a nation simultaneously. Jim wrote this about Carol,

Carol had a radical confidence in God. She always knew He would come through. When I was struggling with theological questions, she totally believed Him. She was like a spiritual rock to me! …[Nothing]"shook" her or her faith. She was resolved that God was God right to her last breath. I never saw her waver once in 42 years.

And she was remarkable at meeting the full range of needs for every family member…Carol knew how to truly "complete" me—exactly the way the Bible says we are supposed to complete each other: emotionally, intellectually, physically, sexually, psychologically, and spiritually. That is the reason that we became—with the passing of years—more madly in love…

She taught a course on "Sexual Fulfillment in Marriage" based on Song of Solomon. (After she passed away, I chose to keep all her notes from this class.) She began teaching it without me really knowing much about what she was saying. I was too busy pastoring. Then one day a young husband greeted me at the church door after a service with a big smile on his face. He said, "Hey, I don't know exactly what your wife is teaching my wife in that class, but tell her to 'Keep teaching it'!"

I decided to find out what my wife was saying in that class. And—speaking as a man—it was great!

She taught the women how to understand their husbands and how to help make sexual intimacy special times of creativity, ingenuity, and spontaneity. Husbands love to be surprised by unanticipated sexual encounters with their wives. That draws every husband to his wife…I once made this statement publically: "Sex is God's idea and, second to salvation, it is the best idea He ever had!" I have a theory. Some people say, "Well, sex is not all that important; you must have the spiritual component." Well, no doubt, the spiritual commitment to Christ must be the foundation of a marriage, but here is what Carol and I discovered…

In the hard times…"both the spiritual and the sexual held us together." When cancer hit, we virtually had no conflict for the last six years of her life…Our great marriage became even greater. We had always had a great marriage BC (before cancer), but it became remarkable AD (after disease).

The last words she heard from me were "I love you." At 9:03 Sunday morning, April 21, 2013, she responded, "I love you." That was our final exchange. I held her until she breathed her last—and for some time after that. I stood in awe of her for 42 years. I stand in awe of her even more now that she is gone.

That's how I want to be remembered and cherished by my husband. How about you?

> *Let it be the hidden person of the heart, with the imperishable quality of a gentle and quiet spirit, which is precious in the sight of God* (1 Peter 3:4.).

♥ Tips for Red-Hot Romance ♥

Don't let the "quiet spirit" aspect in 1 Peter 3:4 fool you. It's referring to what happens in *public*. What happens in private is something else altogether! Let's look at the Shulammite bride who had a successful, yet quiet way of inviting her husband to a sexual encounter: "My beloved has gone down to his garden, to the beds of balsam, to pasture his flock in the gardens and gather lilies" (Song of Solomon 6:2-3). In Song of Solomon, "garden" and gardening terms are all code for the woman's sexuality and body parts. Here are some subtle ways to tell your man "I want you—now!"

A not-so-subtle hint. One man shared his wife's quiet code: "On times when we were leaving town to go to a hotel, she would plan the 'surprise' of a new negligee… She would intentionally leave the skimpy, see-through garment conspicuously laying on the side of the suitcase where I would see it…Obviously she had a clear intent to tantalize—and she succeeded!"

Special socks. One year for Christmas I saw some tennis socks that flipped up for "tonight" and down for "not tonight." I thought I was being sly by placing them at the bottom of Bill's Christmas stocking. However, when the family gathered, Bill dumped out the entire stocking. He spotted the socks, smiled, and quickly tucked them away—but not quite fast enough! Our son, a newlywed, saw the socks. He leaned over to his dad and said, "Dad, if you need socks to clue you in, I'd be glad to school you up."

Respectful ♥

Becoming a wife who is civil, complimentary, courteous, gracious, polite, and shows regard and reverence to her husband.

One wife of a golfing fanatic surprised him with a golfing vacation. She shared,

> I didn't golf but I tried it anyway. I enjoyed it so much that I took some lessons. Now my husband and I regularly enjoy golfing dates. We're guaranteed two hours of alone time, it's relaxing to walk and talk, and it's great exercise. Plus this is an area

he can teach and mentor me in so it makes him feel great about himself. I always thank him for our together time.

This wife got a "two fer." She enjoyed an activity her husband loves, and she showed him honor while doing it. Are you familiar with the bestselling *Love & Respect* book by Emerson Eggerichs? He wisely captured the need of a husband to consistently feel respect from his wife. In a national survey of 400 men cited in his book, guys were given a choice: "If they were forced to choose…which would they prefer to endure? a) to be left alone and unloved in the world or b) to feel inadequate and disrespected by everyone. Seventy-four percent said they would prefer being alone and unloved in the world."[1]

Dr. Eggerichs continued. "[Your husband] needs sexual release as you need emotional release. This is why he loves the act of sex in and of itself…As a woman, you may feel that the two of you have to feel and be close in order to share sexually. For him, however, it is the reverse; the sexual act is what brings the two of you close!"[2]

[Every husband] must love his wife as he loves himself, and the wife must respect her husband (Ephesians 5:33 NIV).

❧ Tips for Red-Hot Romance ❧

A perfect guy date could be as simple as grilling some red meat and watching a movie that involves sports, spies, motorcycles, transformers, superheroes, fighting, or watching an episode of *Shark Week, Myth Busters, Storm Chasers, Ice Truckers,* or *Duck Dynasty*. Another sure hit for a man would be a date that included bacon-wrapped mini sausages and a Wii or X-box game where you and your guy compete with a guitar, as a member of a military's special forces, or where fantasy football dreams are lived out. (And you get a bonus point if you let him put his feet on the coffee table!)

Humorist Dave Barry summarized romance for each gender:

> *What women want:* to be loved, to be listened to, to be desired, to be respected, to be needed, to be trusted, and sometimes, just to be held.
>
> *What men want:* tickets for the World Series.[3]

I asked Bill and our sons for lists of some of their favorite dates. Here are a few of their replies:

- ♥ Driving go-carts at a racetrack
- ♥ Hiking in Hawaii
- ♥ Skeet shooting or going to a gun range
- ♥ Wakeboarding or waterskiing

- ♥ Snow skiing or snowboarding
- ♥ Going to a car show
- ♥ Attending a jazz festival (listen to different bands and choose from different foods)
- ♥ A good hamburger place (with manly ingredients that include bacon, onions, peppers, cheese, barbeque sauce, and extra beef patties)
- ♥ "Sex for dessert" restaurants (fancy places a wife appreciates so she gets "in the mood")

Men might also like a trip to the driving range, bowling alley, deer blind, NASCAR track, lake (with fishing gear, sailboat, or powerboat), or a whitewater river (with a kayak or raft). Kathi Lipp, in *The Marriage Project*, offers more ideas, including this one suggested by a pastor: "Another date that I've wanted to try is a wind tunnel where they simulate skydiving. It's a good date as long as the woman doesn't mind messing up her hair." [4] Another guy, Doug, suggested, "Paintballing." (Skip says, "There is nothing sexier than a woman in camo.") [5]

Audience members have given us some guy-friendly date ideas too:

- ♥ "I bought my husband an 'intake manifold' for his race car. He says it is the most romantic thing I have done for him!"

♥ "My mom came over and suggested my husband and I go for ice cream and she'd watch the kids. However, when I missed the turn for ice cream and he became inquisitive, I gestured toward a bag I had packed—complete with a T-shirt sporting his college logo. We were headed out of town for the big rival game—a perfect romantic date for him: football and his girl!"

♥ "For my husband's thirtieth birthday I created and numbered 30 cards. I hid them around the house each day like a countdown. The cards culminated with '4 hours with our daughter who loves you,' '3 days alone anytime this year for a guy activity,' '2 days in Chicago with me,' and '1 night with me at a hotel!'"

♥ "I planned a 'Pirate 50th birthday' complete with appropriate decorations and costumes. I then 'stole' his sailboat, packed him up, and we 'sailed away' with me as his 'captive.'"

♥ "I bought some cute 'little' camo clothes (my husband loves to hunt). I waited 'til deer season and asked my husband to go with me to the woods and deer hunt. We woke up early, and I put on my warm hunting clothes. I sat very quietly with him in the woods. We went home for lunch, and I showed my husband the pretty, 'little' camo nightie I had on under my hunting outfit. I told my honey, 'You can hunt whitetail at home anytime. You don't need to go to the woods to see your "dear." ' "

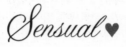

Becoming a wife who is able and willing to gratify her husband's senses or appetite; who is luscious, delectable, delicious, scrumptious, and erotically enamored with her man.

Sue and Jeff Duffield travel extensively as recording artists singing at "Date Nights." Couples listen to their romantic CD *Standard Response* to set the mood for romance. Sue and Jeff have a simple love code. Sue wrote, "Jeff and I love York Peppermint Patties. It's a great 'kissing' exchange. If I want to get Jeff started, all I have to do is hide a York Peppermint Patty in his pocket or briefcase." Try it. Place the edge of a patty between your lips and then share a kiss…and some sweet, chocolate, minty love.

"Let him kiss me with the kisses of his mouth—for your love is more delightful than wine" (Song of Solomon 1:2 NIV).

♥ Tips for Red-Hot Romance ♥

Let's take a peek at King Solomon's wife (let's call her "Red-Hot Wife"—RHW). Here's our spin on some of the creativity RHW showed and her impact on some wives today (as shared by them).

RHW: "Let us rise early and go to the vineyards... There I will give you my love" (Song of Solomon 7:12). (She is inviting her husband to have sex outside.)

Today's wife: "I read in Song of Songs about making love in the vineyard, so when my husband and I traveled to an island and were backpacking far away from any people, I pulled my husband onto a bed of jungle leaves!"

RHW: "And over our doors are all choice fruits, both new and old, which I have saved up for you, my beloved" (Song of Solomon 7:13). (She is open to sex in two ways: traditional and new ways.)

Today's wife: "The kids think it is just a gazebo for

the Jacuzzi with a wide set of benches [the 'old'], but when they are away it is our bed outside ['new' romance]!"

RHW: "Hurry, my beloved, and be like a gazelle or a young stag" (Song of Solomon 8:14). (She is telling him, "Hurry up! I need sex now!")

Today's wife: "We hiked up a secluded mountain mid-week, and when we hit the summit I said, 'An accomplishment this great needs rewarded!' I spotted a cleft in some rocks and invited my husband to make love. We still smile anytime we hear the words 'peak performance.'"

RHW: "How handsome you are, my beloved! Oh, how charming! And our bed is verdant" (Song of Songs 1:16 NIV).

Today's wife: "I wanted to replicate a 'verdant' bed. I learned that meant it was lush like an oasis, so I created a secret hideaway bed in our garden!"

RHW: "Let his left hand be under my head and his right hand embrace me" (Song of Solomon 2:6).

Today's wife: "The bride in Song of Songs gave tactful direction, sharing what she liked. If you want, you can guide your husband's hands or say, 'Try this and let's see what happens.' Let him know if something he is doing is pleasing you. Let your body language send the message, 'That's the way (ahuh, ahuh) I like it!'"

RHW: "My beloved is white and ruddy, chief among ten thousand" (Song of Solomon 5:10 NKJV).

Today's wife: We appreciate Dr. David Jeremiah's book *What the Bible Says About Love, Marriage and Sex*, a commentary on Song of Songs. The meaning of the word "white" in the RHW quote is better captured as "dazzling" or "spectacular."[1] Make a list of how your man stands out from the crowd. Use an online "word art" program and spin his best traits into a photo to post on his desk or turn it into a card to mail to him.

RHW: "My beloved has gone down to his garden, to the beds of balsam, to pasture his flock in the gardens" (Song of Solomon 6:3). ("Pastures his flock among the lilies" is a euphemism for sex.)

Today's wife: Here are a few codes you can use from our book *Red-Hot Monogamy*: 1) Write on the steamy bathroom mirror a number from 1 to 10 indicating how amorous you're feeling. Explain that 1 means "Come home at lunch!"; 2) While giving a seminar, Bill and I noticed the adults referred to sex on the sly by saying, "We come home early." 3) One woman moves a heart magnet on the refrigerator. The closer to the top, the more she wants her man.

Becoming a wife who anticipates the needs and wants of others and is attentive, considerate, helpful, hospitable, caring, compassionate, sympathetic, tender, courteous, gracious, polite, diplomatic, tactful, charitable, and generous.

We want our love to be consistent through life. Red-hot wives are considerate of what their husbands are feeling and processing at any given life stage. We look for ways to turn obstacles into opportunities to love. One bride shared this innovative solution to a very common problem:

My husband has sleep apnea, and I have rheumatoid arthritis. We've decided it's easier to sleep apart. I suggested to my husband that we should have sex every morning before work. He loved the idea!

Let's reflect on God's blueprint for love to help make plans on how we can thoughtfully express our love to our husbands:

> Love never gives up. Love cares more for others than for self. Love doesn't want what it doesn't have. Love doesn't strut, doesn't have a swelled head, doesn't force itself on others, isn't always "me first," doesn't fly off the handle, doesn't keep score of the sins of others, doesn't revel when others grovel, takes pleasure in the flowering of truth, puts up with anything, trusts God always, always looks for the best, never looks back, but keeps going to the end (1 Corinthians 13:3-7 MSG).

Which trait of love do you want to focus on during this season?

♥ Tips for Red-Hot Romance ♥

Be brave. Dr. Lisa Masterson, MD (ob/gyn), shares that up to half of sexually active couples use some kind of vaginal lubricant. A lubricant can help alleviate pain for the newlywed, the young mom after giving birth, and aid a midlife woman dealing with dryness. Many lubricants can be purchased over the counter at your local pharmacy, but you sometimes need to courageously ask for a case to be unlocked.

Be consistent. "The simple truth of erectile dysfunction (ED) is that men need to use their erections or risk losing them." Dr. Masterson reminds women that "the vagina is a muscle, and if you don't use it, it will shrink."[1] Make sex with your husband a priority.

Be understanding. There will be times he can't perform. (If he is tired, preoccupied, stressed, feeling pressured, or if you just had sex, he may not be able to—yet.) This is common and isn't labeled impotence until his failure to maintain (or achieve) an erection happens more than 50 percent of the time.[2] Give your man plenty of affirmation. Ejaculation isn't the goal; closeness is.

Be a team. You may need to look for alternative ways to arousal. "Seventy-five percent of women...do not have orgasm by [vaginal] sex alone."[3] In addition, as you age, traditional methods of sex may need to be replaced by other forms of affection. Make an appointment with your medical doctor. You and your spouse need to tackle any issue together so it won't keep you apart.

Unselfish ♥

Becoming a wife who is charitable, openhanded, altruistic, benevolent, humanitarian, philanthropic, compassionate, and sympathetic.

When I was trying to capture the attributes of an unselfish wife, the synonyms all seemed to lead to the same source: the *heart* (great-hearted, large-hearted, freehearted, open-hearted, goodhearted). This reminds me of a teaching I learned as a little girl: "A good [woman] brings good things out of the good stored up in [her] heart" (Luke 6:45 NIV). An unselfish heart will blossom and put forth unselfish words and actions. The Good Samaritan parable captures the essences of an unselfish heart.

> There was once a man traveling from Jerusalem to Jericho. On the way he was attacked by robbers...A Samaritan traveling the road came on him. When he saw the man's condition, *his heart went out to him.* He gave him first aid, disinfecting and bandaging his wounds (Luke 10:30-34 MSG).

Be like the Good Samaritan by being unselfish with your husband:

- ♥ Pray for him or for the day ahead of him. As you pray, ask God to prompt you to do something to ease your man's tension.

- ♥ Walk through his closet, look in his drawers, scan his desk. Would he appreciate help getting organized?

- ♥ Scan his body head to toe. Would his stress be eased by a massage? Sharon Jaynes' book *Praying for Your Husband from Head to Toe* may help you increase your desire for your husband.

- ♥ Get into his car. Would driving be easier for him if you added an accessory, cleaned, or fixed something?

- ♥ Could your husband benefit from a "quickie"? Dr. Juli Slattery says men prefer "quantity over quality." [1] If you're looking for a few ways to work a quickie into your schedule, try waking him up a little early, asking him to come home at lunch, making use of the baby's naptime, offering to bring him to climax with your hands, waking him up in the middle of the night, or jumping into the shower with him.

Liz Sanchez decided to create a "Pretty Nightie Challenge," by wearing something pretty to bed for 30 days. "Do you know what happened the first night I slipped into bed with a pretty nightie on? He first asked why I was wearing it…[then] he snuggled me up to him and said, 'Oh, wow. That means I get to have my wife as I've always wished to have her!'" [2]

Consider the kind of extravagant love the Father has lavished on us (1 John 3:1 VOICE).

♥ Tips for Red-Hot Romance ♥

Climb into your husband's world…

- ♥ Climb over him to get his attention as you get out of bed (or climb onto him to wake him).

- ♥ Climb onto his lap as he is sitting eating breakfast, watching TV, or working in his home office.

- ♥ Climb between him and the steering wheel *after* he parks the car in the garage. Slide the seat back and lean it down, and then go with the mood.

- ♥ Climb the stairs ahead of him at home, leading him as you strip him down.

- ♥ Climb on the back of his motorcycle, horse, surfboard—for some closeness.

Virtuous ♥

Becoming a wife who exhibits moral excellence, Christian ethics, righteousness, honesty, trustworthiness, and upright choices.

The "Plimsoll line" is a mark located on a ship's hull that indicates the maximum depth the vessel may be safely immersed when loaded with cargo. A ship's captain determines the appropriate Plimsoll line needed for a safe voyage.[1] Your husband has a Plimsoll line too. Load him up too much, and his life, health, or your relationship will sink. He needs you to be aware of his Plimsoll line.

Help him avoid overwork, overcommitment, and over-the-top stress. He is responsible for his choices, yes, but most husbands will try to please their wives. So be a woman of virtue and take on this vital Plimsoll task.

We were speaking to college students (both genders), and I said, "Girls, what these guys want is a low-maintenance woman who will lower his stress and raise his ability to succeed. That is what a man thinks is romantic!"

One of my favorite verses in the Bible is a phrase

Boaz says to Ruth (a woman he is interested in): "All my people in the city know that you are a woman of excellence" (Ruth 3:11). The word "excellence" can also be translated "virtue," "valor," and "valiant" in reference to soldiers. You are a "warrior" wife, a defender of your husband, your marriage, and your family.

♥ Tips for Red-Hot Romance ♥

How well do you know what stresses your man? In *Men Are Like Waffles, Women Are Like Spaghetti*, we explain that men and women process stress differently. We women talk our way through stress. Men, on the other hand, go to their favorite "easy box" to rest and recharge. But God helped us women out so we can recognize our husbands' recharger boxes. They are most likely shaped like boxes: the TV, garage, football field, baseball field, basketball court, tennis court, pool table, soccer field, computer, refrigerator, and the bed. In fact, the "bed box," also known as "the sex box," is a favorite box for men to go to when they're stressed. It's like the free square in the middle of a bingo card. They can get there from every square on their life "waffle"! (Bill and I developed a code phrase for wanting sex: "Want to play some bingo?" Just seeing a bingo card in his briefcase or on his desk lowers Bill's stress level.)

Where does your man go when he is stressed? Schedule a visit to his favorite relaxation boxes!

Be a mall hostess. Visit a high-tech store that offers free use of a massage reclining chair.

Be his hot-tub buddy. Join him in the Jacuzzi. Once there, let him take the lead.

Be his geisha. Run a hot bath, light candles, and offer to provide his favorite pleasures.

Be the spa owner. Give him a mani- or pedicure or both. Offer to give him a mud-mask facial (boys and mud have been a winning combination for ages!).

Be his masseuse. Author Kathi Lipp shared this helpful insight:

> When Roger and I were first married, we spent a small fortune at our local bath and body shop. As our collection of oils and lotions grew, we realized that many of the names—Mango Oil, Almond Paste, and Lemon Rub—sounded a lot like our favorite salad ingredients. So when we go on vacation, we make sure to pack the "Salad Kit." [2]

To make the gift of relaxation easier to give, I (Pam) keep a separate basket for each type of relaxation that includes all the supplies needed to enjoy the activity. Having everything ready means your compassion can move into action when your man hits his Plimsoll line.

Wise ♥

Becoming a wife who is known for deep understand-
ing, keen discernment, and sound judgment.

As wise wives, some of our goals are to increase knowl-
edge, gather experience, gain skills, and apply them with
discernment and understanding. For instance, I (Pam)
wear an "UP" bracelet, a wellness tracker that shows me
how much sleep and physical activity I'm getting. One
day an alert popped up on the screen: "Wednesdays
have a way of keeping the UP community up at night.
People tend to pack too much hustle and bustle…into
their Wednesdays." Knowing this, I made a deliberate
effort to plan a mid-week rendezvous with Bill.

Often couples get into a comfortable rhythm of
Saturday night sex or a Sunday afternoon "nap." Basi-
cally sex once a week. If you create a few more options
in your schedule, you'll find you gain a few more inter-
ludes. For example, "Men's testosterone levels are high-
est in the morning," [1] so wisdom says setting aside a
morning or two a week will add variety to your love life.
If youth group is every Tuesday night, take advantage of
your teens being out of the house.

Kathy Collard Miller, author of *When the Honeymoon's Over*, shares, "Since we have an empty nest and we're home a lot together, I love to wear seductive clothing when we're home for a while. I make sure, though, I have some cover up nearby in case the kids Skype us! We've found that afternoon delights suit us best because we're not tired."

The wise woman builds her house (Proverbs 14:1).

♥ Tips for Red-Hot Romance ♥
Get prepared for *red-hot lovin'*!

Mind ready. Many of the authors we've quoted have wonderful resources, conferences, and online communities. United Marriage Encounter has seasoned marriage mentors committed to giving creative insights (such as "argue naked"—it shortens most disagreements greatly!). Listen to Christian radio, TV, podcasts, and read more books (consider placing a romance book in your glove compartment or on your nightstand). Take turns reading to one another.

Bedroom ready. Place in a basket on the nightstand, in your headboard, or in a drawer next to your bed your "red-hot supplies": favorite scented lotions, linen spray for sheets, candles (and matches), lip gloss in his favorite flavor, breath mints or spray, lubricants, massage oils, recorded love songs, tissues or wipes, and hand towels. You might want to include favorite snacks and water bottles. Try to have everything within an arm's reach. (Just seeing this kit makes most husbands salivate!) Take it a step further and prepare a mini "on the go" kit. Put necessary supplies in a baggie and have it readily available in your purse for those spontaneous moments.

Xenophilic ♥

Becoming a wife who is attracted to foreign peoples, cultures, and customs.

"Xenophilic" simply means "an attraction to foreign peoples, cultures, or customs."[1] Bill and I travel worldwide doing relationships ministry, and we collect romantic ideas everywhere. I was speaking at a women's conference in Japan when our children were young, so Bill was holding down the home front. I wanted to do something really special for Bill. I purchased matching silk kimonos, a Japanese lantern, some oriental music, and even learned a few geisha dance moves. When Bill met me at the airport, I gave him a long, luscious kiss and slid a coin from Japan in his front pocket. I whispered in his ear, "Have I got a yen for you!"

I also collect candles from most places we travel, and Bill knows if he walks into a house with candles aglow from all those happy, shared memories, I'll be igniting his desires too. Dennis and Barbara Rainey, in *Rekindling the Romance*, suggests a husband and a wife each have a candle on their nightstands to use to signal their interest.[2] (Try flameless battery or solar candles.)

♥ Tips for Red-Hot Romance ♥

Here are a few ideas from around the globe.

From Singapore. Often a bride and groom will set aside an entire day to travel the city in their wedding attire and take photos together in all their favorite places. Then they create a photo album. Spend a day going to all your favorite hot spots with a camera that has a self-timer and a tripod. Create a photo album. Pick a favorite photo for your husband's desk and yours.

Europe. Many bridges around the world include "love locks." A "love lock" is where a couple goes together, vows undying fidelity, locks a padlock in place on the bridge, and throws away the keys as a symbol of forever love. Go online to find a bridge where this is allowed. There are "love lock" companies online where you can purchase personalized padlocks.

Mexico and South America. Adapt the tradition of brides who wear a blue slip or sew three ribbons (one yellow, one blue, and one red) on their undergarments to symbolize food, money, and passion for your future together.[3] One adaptation idea is to buy a sexy outfit in those colors or pick up brightly colored fiesta ware and serve up a spicy, traditional Mexican dish for dinner. Make sure he knows you are the "hot tamale." Be sure to play some mariachi and/or salsa music.

Middle East. Put up a backyard Bedouin tent. Lay down a Persian rug and add some cushions and pillows. Serve a Middle Eastern meal complete with Arabian music and dancing.

Africa. Create a safari setting by putting up a tent, add mosquito netting over the bed, play African music, and try your skills with tribal movements.

Worldwide wardrobe. Buy sexy styles of dress: a sarong, a grass skirt, a sari, a kimono, a toga, or a brightly colored African print skirt (top optional). Include a temporary henna tattoo and bright and beautiful necklaces and armbands for additional authenticity.

Yummy ♥

Becoming a wife who cooks delicious, appetizing, fla-vorful, savory, scrumptious, succulent foods.

Nothing says "I adore you" like making your man's favorite meal! Marriage educator Gary Chevalier agrees. "We have all heard the old adage, the way to a man's heart is through his stomach. At our house, Andrea spells love T-A-C-O. They are my favorite food, and I know she is...[sending] me a 'signal' when I smell them cooking. Most taco nights end in red-hot romance." (That gives new meaning to salsa!)

Is there such a thing as "sexy" foods? Ava Cadell, a clinical sexologist, says, "Some foods lower inhibitions, some get the blood flowing directly to the geni-talia, and some foods release happy hormones."[1] "A diet that's healthy for you overall will be healthy for your sex life," says Julie Walsh, spokeswoman for the American Dietetic Association.[2]

Let's look at some nutritional aphrodisiacs. Bill and I have summarized some of the benefits, but you can get more details at our website www.Love-Wise.com.

Proteins for a party. Proteins are vital for building muscle mass in men, which translates into rising testosterone levels increasing his ability to sustain an erection, contribute to healthy libido, or contain vitamins or minerals that raise dopamine levels in the brain that trigger arousal. For some foods, it's the way they are eaten that's erotic: lip-smacking ribs, succulent lobster dipped in butter, or the breast of any fowl. Oysters are historically symbolic aphrodisiacs. Red meat and bacon are synonyms of being male. One food editor contended, "When a man sees you take control of a steak, it'll make him think of you taking control in the bedroom later on, and what's sexier than that?"[3] Power-packed proteins include steak, ribs, lamb, oysters, eggs, shrimp, lobster, poultry, nuts, seeds, cold-water fish, and caviar.

Grain goodness: Oatmeal and whole grains are a natural way to boost testosterone and sex drive and orgasm strength in men *and* women.[4]

Fruits for foreplay: Overall fruits are nature's sugar, so their sweetness is a wise replacement for refined sugars that contribute to diabetes and the erosion of sexual virility. Some fruits have a Viagra effect on blood vessels, raise sperm counts, increase stamina, or rev up sex drives. Sweet fruits are mentally associated with sweet sex, while others have shapes that link to sexuality. For example, avocados. This fruit represents both males and females. Cut it open and it is womb shaped, but it was called by the Aztecs the "testicle tree." The fig is a reminder of the first couple's garden wardrobe. We tasted mangos in the Philippines, and they were so juicy we were told they are best eaten naked or in a bath. Fruits to keep on hand include berries, bananas, peaches, watermelon, citrus and tropical fruits, cherries, pomegranate, and grapes.

Veggies for virility. Many of the veggies good for sexuality have a phallic shape. Some veggies make bodies more responsive to stimuli or, historically, have been considered aphrodisiacs: asparagus, sweet potatoes, carrots, ginger, garlic, leeks, onions, scallions, chives, artichokes, olives, salad greens (arugula, spinach, broccoli, Brussels sprouts, kale, cabbage, Swiss chard, bok choy, celery), tomatoes, and truffles (and truffle oil).

Spices for sizzle. Spices are virtually calorie free but sexually potent. Some are symbolic for red-hot sex: chiles and cayenne. In ancient Rome the word "cinnamon" was used interchangeably with sweetheart and darling.[5] Others create fun interactions: honey or agave nectar drizzled on a plate (or elsewhere). Create a sexy spice rack with saffron, chilies, cayenne, vanilla, nutmeg, cinnamon, ginger, honey, and agave nectar.

Desserts and drinks for delight. Unsweetened green tea's antioxidants promote blood flow boosting sexual stamina. [6] Milk and dairy can "do a body good." Most dairy is high in sugar, so look at skim milk, which can boost fertility and lower PMS. [7] Greek yogurt keeps the gut healthy and body lean. Cheese with its protein and calcium are beneficial in *small* servings. Licking an ice cream cone is culinary foreplay. Using whipping cream from a can is too.

Cappuccinos. The female sex drive perks up after a cup of java. [8] Add some sexy cocoa powder sprinkled on top or a heart swirled into the foam and you have "love in a mug." (For extra impact, leave a little foam along your lip line and lick it off s-l-o-w-l-y. However, ingest caffeine sparingly. It is a vasoconstrictor and may have a negative effect on blood flow, lowering libido.) [9]

Dark chocolate. Go for a 70 percent cocoa because it releases the same endorphins triggered by sexual activity! [10] Dark chocolate increases the feelings of attraction between two people and causes a more intense and longer brain buzz than kissing. [11] The Aztecs alleged it invigorated men and loosened the inhibitions of women. For extra sexiness, melt it into a gooey soufflé or use dark chocolate as fondue for strawberries or bananas. (Kiss if you drop anything off your fork into the fondue.)

Your shoots are an orchard of pomegranates with

choice fruits, henna with nard plants, nard and saffron, calamus and cinnamon, with all the trees of frankincense, myrrh and aloes, along with all the finest spices (Song of Solomon 4:13-14).

I have perfumed my bed with myrrh, aloes and cinnamon. Come, let's drink deeply of love till morning (Proverbs 7:17-18 NIV).

♥ Tips for Red-Hot Romance ♥

- ♥ Take a cooking class together.
- ♥ For cooking at home, get a sexy apron, and if you two are alone, wear it only.
- ♥ Make his favorite two foods as a surprise to celebrate him, a special accomplishment, or good news.
- ♥ Have a candlelight picnic in the bedroom, and use your bodies (external only) as the plates.
- ♥ Feed him sensual and erotic foods. Fill him in on the details and aphrodisiacal qualities of each delicacy.

Becoming a wife who makes the most of every moment and exhibits exciting qualities, including gusto, spice, tang, and zing.

"I would say my most effective attention-getter in amazing my husband's hormones is just being playful, flirty, and confident with my nakedness. That's quite a statement for a woman with a way-less-than-perfect body, but I finally believe Bob. He likes it all—the whole thing—every dimple, wrinkle, and lump that shouldn't be there!" says Audrey Meisner, bestselling author of *Marriage Under Cover* and TV host of *My New Day*. She's been married to her cohost, Bob, for 29 years.

My first clue was that I received the most compliments and adoration when I was naked. When I take extra time to get ready, and really get my clothes, makeup, hair, heels, and accessories to the "maybe I really am hot" level, Bob doesn't notice like I hope he would. But then I take those clothes off!

It takes time to be comfortable enough with your

naked body to really play "Adam and Eve," but now when given the chance to be alone with Bob, I can pretty much do anything naked. I sleep naked, clean house, cook, and I definitely do a lot of skinny-dipping. (More accurately, chunky-dunking.) Show off your body as much as you feel comfortable. Take it in stages, add skimpy lingerie with heels, just do as many everyday tasks as possible, wearing as *little* as possible!

So my advice for turning up the heat? Take it all off, and the only thing you have to wear is the attitude "I have something you really want...You can look forward to later, baby!"

Eve, before the fall, had the same attitude Audrey is talking about. "And the man and his wife were both naked and were not ashamed" (Genesis 2:25). Be inspired to put on an "Eve attitude" and get comfortable in your own skin. (Your husband will find your courage a turn-on!) Chances are your man is much more comfortable with your naked body than you are. Dr. Tim LaHaye shared that 60 percent of men ages 45 to 59 gave their wives a perfect "10" for being "physically attractive."[1] Sheila Gregoire cites The Family Research Council's study of married couples for who had the most fun in the bedroom. News flash: It was *not* the single, stick-thin bathing suit models! "The prototypical sexually happy woman better resembled that middle-aged secretary who lives down your street... She has the secret to sexual success: she's been married to the same man for twenty-two years, and they are totally and utterly committed to one another."[2]

One study revealed the second most appealing sexual act for men and women (preceded only by intercourse) was watching a partner undress.[3] So turn *on* the lights and drop the fig leaf like these "Eve with an attitude" women did.

- ♥ "I bought a cute pair of cowboy boots. When I tried them on, I asked my husband what he thought I should wear with them? His smile and answer 'Earrings?' has prompted me to ask that question each time I model something new" (Kendra Smiley, coauthor with husband, John, of *Do Your Kids a Favor...Love Your Spouse*).

- ♥ "I sent the kids away for the night and then challenged my husband to a game of 'strip pool' in our basement...It took me 16 years of marriage to initiate this sort of thing, but he said it was his favorite date night ever—so far!"

- ♥ "There was a time my husband and I had to live with his mother for about six months. I had a balloon delivered to him at work with a hotel key as the weight. When he arrived at the hotel, I greeted him with a 'card' that I had made of two poster boards and me standing between them with nothing but a bow on my head!"

♥ "On my husband's twenty-fifth birthday, I wrapped myself in 25 balloons (with nothing underneath) and handed him a pin as he walked in the door after work!"

Two are better than one, because they have a good return for their labor: If either of them falls down, one can help the other up (Ecclesiastes 4:9-10 NIV).

♥ Tips for Red-Hot Romance ♥

Keep the zest going by creating a network of confident marriage champions.

Zigzag the globe. Make a list of places both of you want to visit. Choose one and make it happen this year.

Encourage others. As Proverbs 27:17 says, "Iron sharpens iron." Socialize as a couple to fortify your love.

♥ Go on a double date with a couple you think has the kind of marriage you want.

- ♥ Invite an older couple over for dinner and see if they would be willing to mentor you.

- ♥ Get to know your pastor or a clergy couple.

- ♥ Join a marriage-centered, small-group study.

- ♥ Invite some couples from church or from your extended family to come over for a meal.

Sister or mentor each other. Fawn Weaver, founder of the "Happy Wives Club," says, "Happily ever after is not a fairy tale. It's a choice."[4] Fawn started a website connecting wives. When you find other wives who are happily married and enjoy their husbands, get together with them often. Share dating ideas and pray for each other's marriages.

Talk to God. Pray together daily as a couple. Why not try praying naked? Sit face-to-face, bodies entwined, and pray for each other while you look into each other's eyes. You can also pray for your husband silently as you make love. This will increase your zest for him! This is *real* intimacy—the meeting of body, soul, and spirit as God intended, creating pure passion and romance that stays red hot.

Notes ♥

Beautiful

1. Carolyn Coker Ross, MD, "Why Do Women Hate Their Bodies?" http://psychcentral.com/blog/archives/2012/06/02/why-do-women-hate-their-bodies/, 6/2/12, accessed 9/3/13.

2. "Media Influence," http://www.raderprograms.com/causes-statistics/media-eating-disorders.html, accessed 9/3/13.

3. "Dying to Be Barbie," http://www.rehabs.com/explore/dying-to-be-barbie/#.UejZmY3VCSo, accessed 9/10/13.

4. Vicki Heath, seminar at First Place 4 Health, wellness week 2013, www.firstplace4health.com

Expressive

1. Les and Leslie Parrott, *Trading Places* (Grand Rapids, MI: Zondervan, 2008), 79.

2. Gary Smalley, *The DNA of Relationships* (Wheaton, IL: Tyndale, 2004), 96.

3. William Harley, quoted in Tim and Beverly LaHaye, *The Act of Marriage After 40* (Grand Rapids, MI: Zondervan, 2000), 97.

4. Mark Driscoll, *Real Marriage* (Nashville: Thomas Nelson, 2012), 266.

5. Eryn-Faye Frans, LLB, *The Essential Elements of Sex* (Bloomington, IN: iUniverse, 2012), 17.

6. David Schnarch, *Passionate Marriage* (New York: Holt and Company, 1997), 157.

7. Dr. Gary and Barbara Rosberg, with Ginger Kolbaba, *The 5 Sex Needs of Men and Women* (Carol Stream, IL: Tyndale, 2006), 106.

8. Stephen Covey, *7 Habits of Highly Effective People* (New York: Free Press, 1989), 238.

Fun

1. Dave Clarke, *Kiss Me Like You Mean It*, quoted in Arlene Pellicane, *31 Days to a Happy Husband* (Eugene, OR: Harvest House, 2012), 166.

2. Theresa Tamkins, "Wearing Red May Boost Sex Appeal," October 28, 2008, http://news.health.com/2008/10/28/wearing-red-boost-sex-appeal/, accessed 9/10/13.

Good

1. "Good" in Sanskrit is *gadhya*, http://www.merriam-webster.com/dictionary/good, accessed 9/10/13.

2. J.M. Gottman, *Why Marriages Succeed or Fail: And How to Make Yours Last* (New York: Simon and Schuster, 1994), 41.

3. Ibid., 41-42, italics in original.

Humble

1. Juli Slattery, PhD, "Helping Your Husband Become a Leader," interview by Nancy Leigh DeMoss, "Revive Our Hearts," January 24, 2013, http://www.reviveourhearts.com/radio/revive-our-hearts/helping-your-husband-become-leader/, accessed 9/4/2013.

2. Kevin Leman, PhD, *Sheet Music* (Carol Stream, IL: Tyndale, 2003), 52.

Interesting

1. Douglas Rosenau, quoted in Juli Slattery and Linda Dillow, *Passion Pursuit: What Kind of Love Are You Making?* (Chicago: Moody, 2013), 158.

Joyful

1. Roko Belic, dir., *Happy*, 2011, documentary on happiness, Creative Visions Foundation and Wadi Rum Production, www.thehappymovie.com, accessed 9/10/13.

2. Ed Wheat, MD, and Gaye Wheat, *Intended for Pleasure* (Grand Rapids, MI: Revell/Baker, 1977), 220.

Kind

1. John and Anita Renfroe, *Duets: Still in the Word...Still in the Mood* (Colorado Springs: David C. Cook, 2010), 176-77.

Loving

1. Kevin Leman, PhD, *Sheet Music* (Wheaton, IL: Tyndale, 2003), 144.

2. Dr. Gary and Barbara Rosberg, with Ginger Kolbaba, *The 5 Sex Needs of Men and Women* (Carol Stream, IL: Tyndale, 2006), 134-35.

3. Arlene Pellicane, *31 Days to a Happy Husband* (Eugene, OR: Harvest House, 2012), 31.

4. Eryn-Faye Frans, LLB, *The Essential Elements of Sex* (Bloomington, IN: iUniverse, 2012), 19.

5. Quoted in Gary Smalley and Ted Cunningham, *The Language of Sex* (Ventura, CA: Regal Books/Gospel Light, 2008), 159.

6. Tony and Alisa DiLorenzo, *7 Days of Sex Challenge* (San Diego: 2012), 5-6.

7. Rosberg and Rosberg, *5 Sex Needs*, 180.

8. Sheila Gregoire, "29 Days to Great Sex," Love, Honor, and Vacuum blog, http://tolovehonorandvacuum.com/2012/02/29-days-to-great-sex-day-1-the-act-of-marriage/, accessed 9/5/13.

Moral

1. "Good Food for Better Sex," citing research by Alan R. Hirsch, MD, FACP, Smell and Taste Treatment and Research Foundation (Chicago), http://www.webmd.com/menopause/features/good-food-for-better-sex?page= 2, accessed 9/5/13.

2. "Scents That (Really!) Seduce Him," *Cosmopolitan*, http://www.cosmopolitan.com/hairstyles-beauty/skin-care-makeup/scents-that-seduce, accessed 9/5/13.

3. Kassidy Emmerson, " 6 of the Sexiest Candle Fragrances that Will Heat Up Your Love Life," June 26, 2012, http://voices.yahoo.com/6-sexiest-candle-fragrances-will-heat-11494898.html, accessed 9/6/13.

Optimistic

1. Adapted from, Juli Slattery, PhD, *No More Headaches* (Carol Stream, IL: Tyndale, 2009), 17.

Passionate

1. Jay and Laura Laffoon, *He Said. She Said.* (Ada, MI: Baker Books, 2010), 156-57.

2. Mehmet Oz, MD, blog entry from "You, the Owner's Manual," http://www.sharecare.com/health/sex-and-relationships/health-benefits-of-male-masturbation, accessed 9/10/13.

Respectful

1. Emerson Eggerichs, PhD, *Love & Respect* (Nashville: Thomas Nelson, 2004), 49.

2. Ibid., 253.

3. Dave Barry, *Dave Barry's Guide to Marriage and/or Sex* (Emmaus, PA: Rodale Books, 2000), v.

4. Kathi Lipp, *The Marriage Project* (Eugene, OR: Harvest House, 2009), 60.

5. Ibid.

Sensual

1. Dr. David Jeremiah, *What the Bible Says About Love, Marriage and Sex* (San Diego: Turning Point, 2010), 193.

Thoughtful

1. Lisa Masterson, MD (ob/gyn), *The Doctors*, TV show taped in Hollywood, http://www.thedoctorstv.com/main/content/Erectile_Dysfunction, accessed 9/9/13.

2. Ed Wheat, MD, and Gaye Wheat, *Intended for Pleasure* (Grand Rapids, MI: Fleming Revell, 1977), 125.

3. Lisa Masterson, MD (ob/gyn), *The Doctors*, TV show taped in Hollywood, brackets in original, http://www.thedoctorstv.com/main/content/Penis_Size, accessed 9/9/13.

Unselfish

1. Juli Slattery, PhD, *No More Headaches* (Carol Stream, IL: Tyndale, 2009), 80.

2. Liz Sanchez, "Take the Pretty Nightie Challenge," http://www.momlifetoday.com/2010/12/take-the-pretty-nightie-challenge/, accessed 9/9/13.

Virtuous

1. "A commercial ship is properly loaded when the ship's waterline equals the ship's Plimsoll line," http://oceanservice.noaa.gov/facts/plimsoll-line.html, accessed 9/9/13.

2. Adapted from Kathi Lipp, *The Marriage Project* (Eugene, OR: Harvest House, 2009), 129.

Wise

1. "Dr. Ruth's Sex Tips," on *The Doctors*, TV show taped in Hollywood, http://www.thedoctorstv.com/main/content/Dr_Ruth_Sex_Tips, accessed 9/9/13.

Xenophilic

1. "Xenophilic," http://dictionary.reference.com/browse/xenophilic, accessed 9/9/13.

2. Dennis and Barbara Rainey, *Rekindling the Romance: Loving the Love of Your Life* (Nashville: Thomas Nelson, 2004), 258.

3. The Knot, "Wedding Customs: Wedding Traditions from Around the Globe," http://wedding.theknot.com/wedding-planning/wedding-customs/articles/wedding-customs-and-traditions-from-around-the-globe.aspx#ixzz2bVsZ3Zdm, accessed 9/11/13.

Yummy

1. Ava Cadell, PhD (clinical sexologist), "Sexiest Foods," She Knows Food & Recipes, http://www.sheknows.com/food-and-recipes/articles/ 813240/ 10-seductive-foods- 1, accessed 9/9/13.

2. Julie Walsh, MS, RD, quoted in Dulce Zamora, "Good Food for Better Sex?" http://www.webmd.com/menopause/features/good-food-for-better-sex, accessed 9/9/13.

3. Kelsey Harkness, food and wellness editor, Fox News, "15 Sexy Foods to Order on a Date," June 03, 2012, http://magazine.foxnews.com/food-wellness/15-sexy-foods-order-date#ixzz2axadhKMu, accessed 9/9/13.

4. *Men's Health*, Sex MD, "Oatmeal and Whole Grains," "How to Eat for Better Sex" http://www.menshealth.com/sex-md/better-sex-diet, accessed 9/9/13.

5. Cook to Seduce, "Sexy Spices—Use Them!," Nov. 16, 2012, http://cooktoseduce.com/sexy-spices-and-how-to-use-them/, accessed 9/9/13.

6. *Men's Health*, Sex MD, "Green Tea," "How to Eat for Better Sex," accessed 9/9/13.

7. *Health*, "The Amazing Benefits of Milk," in "Foods to Fuel Your Body," http://www.health.com/health/gallery/0,,20307105_3,00.html, accessed 9/9/13.

8. *Women's Health,* "Coffee," "Sexy Foods: The Hot New Meal," http://www.womenshealthmag.com/weight-loss/sexy-foods?page=1, accessed 9/9/13.

9. Katherine Lee, "Rev Up Your Libido," http://www.everydayhealth.com/sexual-health-pictures/healthy-habits-for-a-better-sex-life.aspx#/slide- 7, accessed 9/ 9/ 13; Fruits and Vegetables World, "Sex Life and 10 Top Foods to Boost It," http://fruits-veges.blogspot.com/ 2010/ 08/sex-life-and- 10-top-food-to-boost-it.html, accessed 9/9/13.

10. *Women's Health,* "Chocolate," in "Sexy Foods," accessed 9/9/13.

11. *Men's Health,* "Dark Chocolate," in "How to Eat for Better Sex," accessed 9/9/13.

Zestful

1. Tim and Beverly LaHaye, *The Act of Marriage After 40* (Grand Rapids, MI: Zondervan, 2009), 76.

2. Sheila Wray Gregoire, *The Good Girls Guide to Sex* (Grand Rapids, MI: Zondervan, 2012), 16.

3. Linda Dillow and Juli Slattery, *Passion Pursuit: What Kind of Love Are You Making?* (Chicago: Moody, 2013), 177, quoting a study by the National Opinion Research Center, University of Chicago.

4. Fawn Weaver, "Happy Wives Club," quotes, http://www.happywivesclub.com/marriage-quotes/, accessed 9/10/13. "Happy Wives Club is an upbeat blog dedicated to positively changing the tone about marriage around the world" (Fawn Weaver).

Red-Hot Monogamy

Discover the keys to making and keeping your marriage exciting, growing, and adventurous! With sensitivity and playfulness, the Farrels offer:

- ♥ specific suggestions for making your marriage sizzle
- ♥ communication skills to improve your togetherness
- ♥ guidance on difficult-to-discuss topics

Offering biblical truths on your God-given sexuality, insights into the needs and desires of both genders, and suggestions through true stories, the full-size, 224-page *Red-Hot Monogamy* reveals how you can keep the romance fire burning hot or, if needed, rekindle the embers.

♥ ♡ ♥

To contact the Farrels and learn more about their offered resources, check out these sources:

www.Love-Wise.com

Love-Wise
3755 Avocado Boulevard, #414
LaMesa, CA 91941

800-810-4449

info@Love-Wise.com

Facebook and Twitter